A Paper House

HORACE WALPOLE AT STRAWBERRY HILL

ANNA CHALCRAFT

DRAWINGS BY SYLVIA JONES

✦✦✦

© Anna Chalcraft 1998
Anna Chalcraft asserts the moral right to be identified as the author of this work.

Designed by Annette Peppis. Telephone 0181-943 2701

Published by Highgate of Beverley
Highgate Publications (Beverley) Limited
24 Wylies Road, Beverley, HU17 7AP
Telephone 01482-866826

Produced by ba print
4 Newbegin, Lairgate, Beverley, HU17 8EG
Telephone 01482-886017

British Library Cataloguing in Publication Data.
A catalogue record for this book is available from the British Library.
ISBN 0 948929 33 2

CONTENTS

✠ ✠ ✠

4

THE DRAWINGS

5

TEXTUAL CONVENTIONS

7

THE LETTERS

131

ACKNOWLEDGEMENTS

133

DRAMATIS PERSONAE

137

A SELECT BIBLIOGRAPHY

140

ROOM PLANS OF STRAWBERRY HILL

143

INDEX

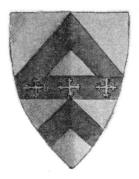

THE DRAWINGS

❖ ❖ ❖

With one exception the drawings are taken from existing 18th and 19th century Gothic detail found at Strawberry Hill, the painted glass within the house, or from objects in the rooms; the exception is the drawing of Horace which is copied from the portrait of 1758 by Allan Ramsay which now hangs in the Lewis Walpole Library, Farmington, Connecticut, and which has been copied with the kind permission of the Librarian.

Architectural Detail: 10, 14, 19, 23, 25, 28, 32, 44, 52, 57, 60, 63, 65, 70, 73, 78, 87, 89, 90, 93, 95, 103, 107, 108, 114, 117, 126

Ceramics: 81

Chimney-pieces and their detail: 41, 47, 49, 55, 123, 128

Furniture: 50, 98

Garden: 35, 67

Heraldic Devices: 3, 11, 20, 30, 36, 110,

Horace, from the painting by Allan Ramsay: 8

Painted Glass detail: 12, 15, 16, 22, 33, 38, 39, 43, 48, 58, 75, 76, 77, 82, 84, 97, 101, 105, 111, 112, 115, 119, 121, 125

Plans: 140, 141

Wallpaper and Paint effects: 26, 68

Textual Conventions

✦ ✦ ✦

Throughout the text the following conventions have been followed:

Spelling of proper names has been standardised throughout.
Spelling, grammar and use of capitals in quotations from Walpole's writing is that used by him.
.....   denotes edited text of letter.
"   "   denotes Walpole's letters or a quotation from his work.
[   ]   denotes an amendment to Walpole's text by the author.
'   '   denotes all other quotations and some foreign terms.
The use of Italics signify the titles of works by Walpole.

*T*his book is compiled around a selection of 18th century letters written by Horace Walpole to his friends. In most of them he discusses his life in Twickenham and the building of his house, Strawberry Hill, one of the most extraordinary houses ever built. The letters reveal that the difficulties of building a house in the 18th century were little different from those faced today – problems with workmen, strikes and delays, shortage of money, and a desire to use the most modern techniques. When it was finished he showed off his house first to friends and then to the public at large to whom he issued tickets. His enjoyment in life and pride in his house shine through the letters as does his humanity, wit and charm. He spent almost fifty years in building Strawberry Hill and in acquiring the extraordinary collection of objects it was built to house.

A few letters on national and international events have been included in the selection in order to paint the background against which he was building and these are integral to understanding the man and his life at Strawberry Hill.

Several times in his letters Walpole writes "My castle is of paper". Not only is a great part of it made of papier-mâché but it is also a paper creation in both a literary and an artistic sense: he designed the building from collections of engravings on paper showing the early Gothic tombs, and from drawings by his friends Richard Bentley and John Chute. He publicised his house on his private printing press, making certain that it was seen, understood and appreciated as he wished. He used the house as a setting for the castle in his novel, *The Castle of Otranto*. In letters to his friends he built up a picture of a castle rather than a house. Strawberry, with its fake medieval exterior, mock monastic cloisters and painted hall are all formed into a castle through Walpole's writing, particularly through the letters and through a published catalogue of contents entitled *A Description of the villa of Mr. Horace Walpole at Strawberry Hill, near Twickenham* which Walpole kept updated. He told the public how they should view it and what they should think: as a publicist he excelled.

✢ ✢ ✢

Part of the importance of Strawberry Hill lies in the wealth of written detail describing its construction, in the fact that the house still stands and may be visited and also that it is possibly the best documented of all 18th century houses. From 1747 Walpole and his friends corresponded frequently discussing styles, plans, craftsmen, furniture and commented on the progress made in building. The details mentioned by them in their letters can be compared with the dated household accounts and with the *Description*. He wrote this document in only five months and published it in 1774 for his friends, updating it ten years later; it lists every item in the house that he considered of any importance. A first, undated copy (possibly also of 1774), was for a cousin, Anne Seymour

Damer, this copy is less complete. In 1800, three years after Walpole's death, a travel guide to Strawberry Hill, the 'Ambulator', was published which again lists all the principal articles within the rooms. A piece of furniture or painted glass can therefore be traced from its origin in a letter through its development and completion; sometimes its movement can even be followed from room to room as tastes changed. In the 19th century the contents were sold at auction by the owner, the 7th Earl Waldegrave, and the sale catalogue listing the contents is another document tracing the development of the interiors. Add to this the wealth of 18th and 19th century engravings and watercolours that exist showing exteriors and interiors of Strawberry Hill, and its importance as a well documented building may be understood.

❖ ❖ ❖

Horatio, or Horace, born in 1717, was the youngest son of Robert Walpole and his wife Catherine Shorter. He was educated at Eton, where he was happy and made many friends, and at King's College Cambridge which he left in 1739, without a degree, to make the Grand Tour with his schoolfriend, Thomas Gray. The young men spent two years travelling together through France and Italy, made a lengthy stay in Florence, eventually quarrelled and returned to England separately. Many of Horace Walpole's letters describing his life in Twickenham were written to friends he had met whilst making the Grand Tour; to Horace Mann alone, a distant relation with whom he stayed in Florence, he wrote about 1800 letters throughout his life, although they never met again after Horace returned to England.

His father, Robert Walpole, regarded as the first Prime Minister and created 1st Earl of Orford, died in 1745 and his eldest brother inherited the title. Robert left the lease of his London town house in Arlington Street to Horace, together with £5,000, which with three sinecures became Horace's income. As a youngest son he was very well provided for.

In 1747 shortly after his father's death he came to Twickenham and first rented, and then bought just over a year later in 1749, the cottage dating back to 1698 which the locals called 'Chopp'd Straw Hall' – because, they said, the Earl of Bradford's coachman had built it with money he had saved by feeding the Earl's horses on chopped straw instead of hay. In his *Short Notes* Walpole wrote, "In May 1747 I took a small house near Twickenham for seven years. I afterwards bought it by Act of Parliament (it belonging to minors) and have made great additions and improvements to it. In one of the deeds I found it was called Strawberry Hill."

He rented the house from the Chenevixes; she sold 'toys', beautiful objects and expensive trinkets, in her shop near Charing Cross in London. It obviously pleased Walpole to think that a purveyor of toys should lease him this tiny house which he later called his "baby-house full of playthings". In the first letter he picks up the idea of a plaything-house and turns his meadows and hedges into pieces of bejewelled decoration as if all was in a jewellers' window. This theme was in his mind for many of the early years he spent at Strawberry and crops up in several of his letters.

The early house of 1698 had a frontage of only about seventeen feet, but even so the Chenevixes had thought it necessary to furnish one room as a library, a fact about which Walpole was decidedly disparaging. Much of the early house remains and structural changes made between 1698 and 1747 (most probably around 1720) can be seen in examination of the brickwork in the Hall (now on an interior wall but originally part of the exterior brickwork).

The cottage could be approached by river, which was wider and shallower than today, and had a tiny landing stage. Traffic on the Thames was busy and Twickenham itself was a bustling area with plenty of light industry which used the river. Traffic increased when the area became the fashionable meeting place for society. Anybody, who was anybody, chose to live there, making land expensive and hard to come by – Walpole paid £776.10s.0d. for the initial five acres in which Chopp'd Straw Hall stood.

Most of the neighbouring houses, including that of Alexander Pope, were considerably larger than Chopp'd Straw Hall. Walpole, who loved watching people, became absorbed by the richness of characters living around him, and considered Pope's 'ghost' to be a near neighbour – Pope had died shortly before Walpole moved into Twickenham.

The general area around Strawberry Hill was known for its market gardens and orchards where a selection of soft fruits, mainly strawberries, were grown. Today, local residents say that each spring wild strawberries still come up in their gardens as weeds do elsewhere.

❖ ❖ ❖

The first two letters describe the original house, one is written to his cousin Henry Seymour Conway, the other to a friend. In the letter to Conway he mentions two roads which came to fascinate him. The Thames was very close to Chopp'd Straw Hall, closer than it is today; it was in the 19th century that locks were built up and down river and the banks of the Thames were shored up to contain the river and cut down the likelihood of houses in the area being flooded. In this early letter can be seen the start of a theme that he

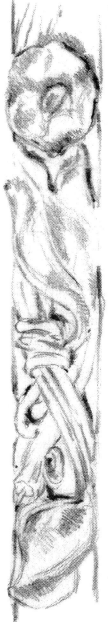

developed with much enjoyment and passion over the years that he lived at Strawberry Hill: Noah. Many of his letters give an exaggerated view of deluges, floods and storms, and several of the painted glass windows which he installed in the house show scenes from the lives of Noah and Neptune.

"To Henry Seymour Conway,   Twickenham, 8 June 1747
You perceive by my date that I am got into a new camp, and have left my tub at Windsor. It is a little play-thing house that I got out of Mrs. Chenevix's shop, and is the prettiest bauble you ever saw. It is set in enamelled meadows, with filigree hedges:
        A small Euphrates through the piece is roll'd
        And little finches wave their wings in gold.
Two delightful roads, that you would call dusty, supply me continually with coaches and chaises: barges as solemn as Barons of the Exchequer move under my window; Richmond Hill and Ham walks bound my prospect; but, thank God! the Thames is between me and the Duchess of Queensberry. Dowagers as plenty as flounders inhabit all around, and Pope's ghost is just now skimming under my window by a most poetical moonlight. I have about land enough to keep such a farm as Noah's, when he set up in the ark with a pair of each kind; but my cottage is rather cleaner than I believe his was after they had been cooped up together forty days. The Chenevixes had tricked it out for themselves: up two pair of stairs is what they call Mr. Chenevix's library, furnished with three maps, one shelf, a bust of Sir Isaac Newton, and a lame telescope without any glasses."

The earliest alterations to Chopp'd Straw Hall and the beginning of its transformation into Strawberry Hill were designed by William Robinson, Secretary to the Board of Works. The first changes were made to the kitchen area and to the room which Walpole used as a Breakfast Room, to which Robinson added a chimney-piece surmounted by an heraldic device of a Saracen's head.

"To C. H. Williams,   Strawberry Hill, 27 June 1748
Dear Sir Charles,
.....You will perceive by the date of my letter that my love for London is wore out; I have got an extreme pretty place just by Twickenham, which I am likely to be pleased with for at least some time, as I have many alterations to make. The prospect is delightful, the house very small, and till I added two or three rooms scarce habitable: at present it will hold as many people as I wish to see here; when you return, I shall be extremely glad to have you of the number....."

George Montagu was a great friend but a bad correspondent answering Walpole's letters only spasmodically over a period of thirty years. In the following extract from a letter to Montagu Walpole starts to paint a picture of the neighbourhood in which he lives.

"To George Montagu,   Strawberry Hill, Saturday night, 3 September 1748 ..... Since I came home I have been disturbed with a strange, foolish woman, that lives at the great corner house yonder; she is the attorney's wife, and much given to the bottle. By the time she has finished that and daylight, she grows afraid of thieves, and makes the servants fire minute guns out of the garret windows. I remember persuading Mrs. Kerwood that there was a great smell of thieves, and this drunken dame seems literally to smell it. .....There are now three more guns gone off; she must be very drunk."

Throughout his time at Strawberry Hill Walpole bought land whenever it became available and it is possible that his building plan, with its Gothic irregularity, was a circumstance partly forced upon him by the strange order in which he was able to acquire land. He was a dedicated gardener creating walks, an avenue of lime trees lining the river view, and a small pool which he called Po-Yang, all to embellish his house. His description of the terrace being on the brow of a natural hill, and the name Strawberry Hill itself, is confusing today, but in the 18th century there was a gentle slope from house to river.

He decided to spend Christmas 1748 at Strawberry Hill although it is apparent from his letters that he originally thought of the house as a summer residence for entertaining and not as a permanent home, and he wrote on Boxing Day to his friend, Horace Mann, discussing his Christmas arrangements in a matter of fact way; decorations of holly coupled with laurel rather than our modern mistletoe or ivy, and he talks of turkey together with beef as being the established food for the feast. The turkey was introduced from the New World and is illustrated, alive, in several 17th century paintings, but here it is obvious that it had already become established as normal English Christmas fare. Walpole may well have seen flocks of wild turkeys in Richmond Park which remained there until removed by George IV in his effort to rid the park of poachers.

Walpole had met Horace Mann in Florence when he was there on the Grand Tour. Mann, a distant relation of the Walpoles, was British Resident in Florence, and always in the thick of news passing between the English nobility abroad. He and Horace Walpole became friends and continued their correspondence until Mann's death. Most of Walpole's letters to Mann set out to document the history of the time and to inform Mann of past and present events about which Walpole believed he, or posterity, should know. Throughout the correspondence these letters are the most political, autobiographical and those most obviously designed for archival purposes.

"To Sir Horace Mann,   Strawberry Hill, 26 December 1748
Did you ever know a more absolute country gentleman? Here am I come down to what you call keep my Christmas! indeed it is not in all the forms; I have stuck no laurel and holly in my windows, I eat no turkey and chine, I have no tenants to invite, I have not brought a single soul with me. The weather is excessively stormy, but has been so warm, and so entirely free from frosts the whole winter, that not only several of my honeysuckles are coming out, but I have literally a blossom upon a nectarine-tree, which I believe was never seen in this climate before on the 26th of December. I am extremely busy here planting; I have got four more acres, which makes my territory prodigious in a situation where land is so scarce, and villas as abundant as formerly at Tivoli and Baiae. I have now about fourteen acres, and am making a terrace the whole breadth of my garden on the brow of a natural hill, with meadows at the foot, and commanding the river, the village, Richmond-hill, and the park, and part of Kingston ....."

Horace Walpole had many visitors at Strawberry Hill, two of the most frequent being Richard Bentley and John Chute. Bentley's father was another Richard Bentley, a notorious but remarkable classicist, who became Master of Trinity College,

Cambridge, and gained fame both for his scholarship and for being the subject of satire by Swift. His son was a gentleman artist and draughtsman who had the misfortune to be married to a woman whom all of his friends seemed to dislike, nicknamed Hecate and Mrs. Tisiphone by Walpole; Bentley was frequently in debt and so short of money that he was often forced to flee his creditors at most inopportune moments leaving work unfinished. Walpole called him "a treasure of taste and drawing", and said of him "he has more sense, judgment and wit, more taste and more misfortunes than sure ever met in any man." The other regular visitor was John Chute whom Walpole had first met on the Grand Tour, and although Chute was sixteen years older than Walpole the men became great friends. Chute, Bentley and Walpole were the founder members of a group known as The Committee, The Committee of Taste, or The Committee on Taste; the Committee consulted books of Gothic engravings and decided as a group what should be done in the building of Strawberry and how it could best be achieved. Much of the early work on the house was designed by Bentley and much of the later, from about 1759, by Chute. Chute's influence on the Committee can be seen in his antiquarian approach to building, based on asymmetry and truth to architectural detail as opposed to Bentley's more fantastic rococo based Gothic style and Walpole's sense of fun. Chute was always Walpole's authority on genealogy and kept heraldic reference books at Strawberry in the Green Closet. Of Chute Walpole wrote "Mr. Chute, whom I have created Strawberry King-at-Arms". None of these three were particularly interested in the structure and stability of the house, this was left to Robinson, and to others. Thomas Gray was another frequent visitor and correspondent with whom the detail of the Strawberry building plans were discussed but he was never admitted to the ranks of the Committee of Taste.

❖❖❖

It is interesting to note that in June 1749 Walpole describes his house to Horace Mann as being pretty but not melancholic. Later he was to include the spirit of chivalry and adventure into his building, but no trace of the spirit of Romantic melancholic loss which became associated with 'Gothic' by the turn of the century. The description of Walpole sitting writing by the Twickenham fireside on a June day, whilst Mann waited to receive the letter in the warmth of Tuscany, creates a wonderful picture of English summertime, but it was rare for Walpole to sit by any fire. After he and the Committee of Taste started work on alterations to the house and designed the new chimney-pieces – made of wood – almost all mention of fires ceases. There are very few descriptions of fires being lit at Strawberry, although there are many descriptions of his friends suffering from the cold. Chimney-pieces were built for theatrical effect and never primarily intended to be of practical use.

"To Sir Horace Mann,   Strawberry Hill, 4 June 1749

As summerley as June and Strawberry hill may sound, I assure you I am
writing to you by the fireside: English weather will give vent to its temper,
and whenever it is out of humour, it will blow east and north and all kinds
of cold. Your brothers Ned and Gal dined with me today, and I carried the
latter back to Richmond: as I passed over the Green, I saw Lord Bath, Lord
Lonsdale and half a dozen more of the White's Club sauntering at the door
of a house which they have taken there, and come to every Saturday and
Sunday to play at whisk. You will naturally ask why they can't play at whisk
in London on those two days as well as on the other five; indeed I can't tell
you, except that it is so established a fashion to go out of town at the end of
the week, that people do go, though it be only into another town. It made
me smile to see Lord Bath sitting there, like a citizen that has left off trade!

Your brother Ned has not seen Strawberry Hill since my great
improvements; he was astonished; it is pretty: you never saw
so tranquil a scene, without the least air of melancholy: I
should hate it, if it was dashed with that .....

Mr. Chute, who went from hence this morning, and is always
thinking of blazoning your pedigree in the noblest colours,
has turned over all my library, till he has tapped a new and
very great family for you: in short, by your mother it is very
clear that you are descended from Hubert de Burgh, grand
justiciary to Richard II: indeed I think he was hanged; but
that is a misfortune that will attend very illustrious genealogies;
it is as common to them as to the pedigrees about Paddington
and Blackheath. I have had at least a dozen great-great-
grandfathers that came to untimely ends. All your virtuosos
in heraldry are content to know that they had ancestors who
lived five hundred years ago, no matter how they died. A match
with a low woman corrupts a stream of blood as long as the
Danube – tyranny, villainy and executions are mere flea-bites
and leave no stain ....."

He decided to put battlements around his roof although they were not completed
until 1752, and to transform the house into a castle. At this stage it was still very
small, not much larger than an English 20th century semi-detached house.

"To George Montagu,   Strawberry Hill, 28 September 1749

I am much obliged to you, my dear Sir, and agree with your opinion about
that painting of Prince Edward that it can't be original, and authentic, and
consequently not worth copying. Lord Chomley is indeed an original! but

who are the wise people that build for him? Sir Philip Hobby seems to be the only person likely to be benefited by this new extravagance. I have just seen a collection of tombs like those you describe; the house of Russell, robed in alabaster and painted; there are seven monuments in all; one is immense, flaunting in marble, cherubim'd and seraphim'd, crusted with bas reliefs and titles, for the first Duke of Bedford and his Duchess. All these are in a chapel of the church at Cheyneys, the seat of the first Earls. There are but piteous fragments of the house remaining, now a farm, built round three sides of a court. It is dropping down, in several places without a roof, but in half the windows are beautiful arms in painted glass. As these are so totally neglected, I propose making a push and begging them of the Duke of Bedford: they would be magnificent for Strawberry Castle. Did I tell you that I have found a text in Deuteronomy, to authorize my future battlements? 'When thou buildest a new house, then shalt thou make a battlement for thy roof, that thou bring not blood upon thy house, if any man fall from thence'. I saw Cheyneys at a visit I have been making to Harry Conway at Latimers. This house which they have hired is large and bad, old but of a bad age; finely situated on a hill in a beech wood, with a river at the bottom, and a range of hills and woods on the opposite side belonging to the Bedford. They are fond of it; the view is melancholy. In the church at Cheyneys, Mr. Conway put on an old helmet we found there; you can't imagine how it suited him, how antique and handsome he looked, you would have taken him for Rinaldo. Now I have dipped you so deep in heraldry and genealogies, I shall beg you to step into the church of Stoke, I know it is not asking you to do a disagreeable thing to call there; I want an account of the tomb of the first Earl of Huntingdon, an ancestor of mine who lies there. I asked Gray but he could tell me little about it. You know how out of humour Gray has been about our diverting ourselves with pedigrees, which is at least as wise as making a serious point of haranguing against the study; I believe neither Mr. Chute nor I ever contracted a moment's vanity from any of our discoveries, or ever preferred them to anything but brag and whisk. Well, Gray has set himself to compute, and has found out that there must go a million of ancestors in twenty generations to everybody's composition –

I dig and plant till it is dark; all my works are revived and proceeding. When will you come and assist? You know I have an absolute promise, and shall now every day expect you. My compliments to your sisters.

I am, dear George, yours most faithfully,

H.W."

In the postscript of the following letter he relates to Mann that he intends to build onto Strawberry in the Gothic style; even at this early stage Gothic architecture and painted glass are paired in his mind. It is obvious that it is the general 'feel' that the glass creates which Walpole believes to be important, rather than any one particular scene or strand – except for the use of heraldic glass with coats of arms. In any context where there may be an element of confusion it has become usual to distinguish between early Gothic, and Walpole's adaptation of the style, as Strawberry Hill Gothic or Gothick 'with a k'.

"To Sir Horace Mann,   Arlington Street, 10 January 1750
I don't at all know what to say to you, for not having writ to you since the middle of November: I only know that nothing has happened, and so I have omitted telling you nothing .....

To make up for my long silence, and to make up a long letter, I will string another old story, which I have just heard ..... General Wade was at a low gaming-house, and had a very fine snuff box, which on a sudden he missed. Everybody denied having taken it: he insisted on searching the company: he did: there remained only one man, who had stood behind him, but refused to be searched, unless the General would go into another room alone with him: there the man told him, that he was born a gentleman, was reduced, and lived by what little bets he could pick up there, and by fragments which the waiters sometimes gave him – 'At this moment I have half a fowl in my pocket; I was afraid of being exposed; here it is! Now, Sir, you may

search me.' Wade was so struck, that he gave the man an hundred pound – and immediately the genius of generosity, whose province is almost a sinecure, was very glad of the opportunity of making him find his own snuff-box, or another very like it, in his own pocket again .....

P.S. My dear Sir, I must trouble you with a commission, which I don't know whether you can execute. I am going to build a little Gothic castle at Strawberry Hill. If you can pick me up any fragments of old painted glass, arms or anything, I shall be excessively obliged to you. I can't say I remember any such thing in Italy, but out of old châteaus I imagine one might get it cheap, if there is any."

Except for writing that he liked irregularity and variety and that he considered that the Classical style of architecture was only suitable for great or public buildings Walpole never really explained why he chose Gothic as a style in which to build: there were almost certainly not one but many reasons which together effected his choice. Shortly before he came to Strawberry Hill to live the Jacobites had attempted a resurgence and been beaten back in a series of defeats culminating in the '45. By 1750 English and Scottish Catholicism was centred in Rome around the followers of the Pretender and posed a real threat to the security of England. Walpole had followed his father into parliament as a whig, committed to upholding the protestant line through the Hanoverian Georges. Possibly Rome with its Classical architecture, a city he disliked, and a hotbed of Stuart unrest, encouraged him to favour an architectural period in which he felt more comfortable. By reverting to the Gothic style of building for a private house, a style which had never completely died out in England, he was returning to a period he may have thought of as being English and Northern European, free from the influence of Rome and the Catholic church. If this is correct then it is perhaps ironic that the original Gothic architecture was built to glorify God through the Catholic church whilst the classical architecture of Rome was pagan or adapted from a pagan model.

However it is simplistic to assume that a man with as many interests as Horace Walpole pursued Gothic for only one reason. He had grown up with great Gothic buildings all around him, and their influence must have been very strong. Strong also was his spirit of nationalism; he had an admiration for the Tudors and the English Renaissance, he treasured a 2nd Folio Shakespeare, miniatures by Oliver and Hilliard, drawings by Holbein, in all of these his Englishness was apparent. There was also the desire that each generation has to renounce the tastes of preceeding generations and find a new style; Horace's father had not only been virtually England's first Prime Minister but he had built Houghton Hall in Norfolk, one of the most magnificent palaces of the 18th century, in the Palladian style. To make his mark Walpole had to build a quite different house – he chose a villa only seventeen feet wide adapted from a lodging house and built of the cheapest materials to contrast with Houghton Hall's formality and classic beauty, built in the finest materials to serve generations.

By choosing Gothic as a style Walpole was free to form his house as he chose, to include or reject strands which pleased or displeased him, and to pick up a style which was already much used, but was not in high fashion, and to make it 'all the rage'. He had another advantage; new techniques and materials enabled him to build in a way that had previously only been used on the greatest and most expensive buildings. For example, the ceiling of the Long Gallery with its expanse of fan vaulting could not have been built in stone without buttressing, even unsupported plaster would have been too heavy. The lightness and pliability of papier-mâché took the use from cathedral vault to domestic interior and changed it from a piece of structure to an element of decoration.

He was also surrounded by examples of Gothic buildings – such as William Kent's Esher Place; Lord Radnor's new Gothic bathhouse, almost next door to Strawberry, was already built before Walpole came to live in the area.

18th century engravings show a number of Gothic buildings along the banks of the Thames at Twickenham, and in 1747, the year Walpole rented Chopp'd Straw Hall, Batty Langley's most influential source book of the Gothic style was reprinted, 'Ancient Architecture Restored and Improved by a Great Variety of Grand and Useful Designs, entirely New in the Gothick Mode for the Ornamenting of Buildings and Gardens'. The middle of the 18th century was a time when antiquarian interest grew in literature and buildings, fostered by more easily obtained editions of past literary works and the availability of books of engravings which could be used as source material. Batty Langley and others set out the principles of Gothic for a revival waiting to become fashionable. It was Walpole who made it fashionable through his attention to detail, his exuberance, his desire to share it with anyone who might be interested, by his single mindedness and above all by his character and position in society.

✥ ✥ ✥

In his letters we often see a man in advance of contemporary political thinking examining accepted practices but not 'toeing' the social or political line. He disapproved of slavery and wrote against it long before Wilberforce denounced the trade or Josiah Wedgwood produced his anti-slavery plaque.

Many of the letters show a general preoccupation with the weather which always pleased him if it was extreme; here the cold summer of '49 is followed by a very mild winter, remarked on and enjoyed by Walpole, who describes the first of a series of earthquakes.

"To Sir Horace Mann,   Strawberry Hill, 25 February 1750
I am come hither for a little repose and air. The fatigue of a London winter, between Parliaments and rakery, is a little too much without interruption for an elderly personage, that verges towards – I won't say what. This accounts easily for my wanting quiet – but air in February will make you smile – yet it is strictly true, that the weather is unnaturally hot: we have had eight months of warmth beyond what was ever known in any other country; Italy is quite north with respect to us! – you know we have had an earthquake. Mr. Chute's Francesco says, that a few evenings before it, there was a bright cloud which the mob called the bloody cloud; that he had been told there never were earthquakes in England, or else he should have known by that symptom that there would be one within a week. I am told that Sir Isaac Newton foretold a great alteration in our climate in the year '50, and that he wished he could live to see it. Jupiter, I think, has jogged us three degrees nearer to the sun; but I don't tell you this for gospel, though I talk as bad astronomy as if I were inspired .....

We have been sitting this fortnight on the African Company. We, the

British Senate, the temple of Liberty, and bulwark of Protestant Christianity, have this fortnight been pondering methods to make more effectual that horrid traffic of selling negroes. It has appeared to us that six and forty thousand of these wretches are sold every year to our plantations alone! – It chills one's blood – I would not have to say that I voted in it, for the continent of America! The destruction of the miserable inhabitants by the Spaniards, was but momentary misfortune, that flowed from the discovery of the new world, compared to this lasting havoc, which it brought upon Africa. We reproach Spain; and yet do not even pretend the nonsense of butchering these poor creatures for the good of their souls! .....

I despise your literati enormously for their opinion of Montesquieu's book. Bid them read that glorious chapter on the subject I have been mentioning, the selling of African slaves. Where did I borrow that? In what book in the world is there half so much with sentiment, delicacy, humanity?

I shall speak much more gently to you, my dear child, though you don't like Gothic architecture. The Grecian is only proper for magnificent and public buildings. Columns and all their beautiful ornaments look ridiculous when crowded into a closet or a cheesecake house. The variety is little, and admits no charming irregularities. I am almost as fond of the Sharawaggi, or Chinese want of symmetry, in buildings, as in grounds or gardens. I am sure whenever you come to England, you will be pleased with the liberty of taste into which we are struck, and of which you can have no idea. Adieu!"

"To Sir Horace Mann,   Arlington Street, 11 March 1750
        'Portents and prodigies are grown so frequent,
                That they have lost their name'
My text is not literally true; but as far as earthquakes go towards lowering the price of wonderful commodities, to be sure we are overstocked. We have had a second, much more violant than the first; and you must not be surprised if by the next post you hear of a burning mountain sprung up in Smithfield. In the night between Wednesday and Thursday last, (exactly a month since the first shock), the earth had a shivering fit between one and two; but so slight that, if no more had followed, I don't believe it would have been noticed. I had been awake, and had scarce dozed again – on a sudden I felt my bolster lift up my head; I thought somebody was getting from under my bed, but soon found it was a strong earthquake, that lasted near half a minute, with a violent vibration and great roaring. I rang my bell; my servant came in, frightened out of his senses: in an instant we heard all the windows

in the neighbourhood flung up. I got up and found people running into the streets, but saw no mischief done: there has been some; two old houses flung down, several chimneys, and much china-ware. The bells rung in several houses. Admiral Knowles, who has lived long in Jamaica, and felt seven there, says this was more violent than any of them; Francesco prefers it to the dreadful one at Leghorn. The wise say, that if we have not rain soon, we shall certainly have more. Several people are going out of town, for it has nowhere reached above ten miles from London: they say, they are not frightened, but that it is such fine weather, 'Lord! one can't help going into the country!' The only visible effect it has had, was on the Ridotto, at which, being the following night, there were but four hundred people. A parson, who came into White's the morning of earthquake the first, and heard bets laid on whether it was an earthquake or the blowing up of powder-mills, went away exceedingly scandalised, and said, 'I protest, they are such an impious set of people, that I believe if the last trumpet was to sound, they would bet puppet-show against Judgement'. If we get any nearer still to the torrid zone, I shall pique myself on sending you a present of cedrati and orange-flower water: I am already planning a terreno for Strawberry Hill."

*C*lassicism was the framework around which the 18th century was built. At school and university conventional education was structured around the classics, the culmination being the Grand Tour, which young men made much as they went up to Oxford or Cambridge. Going to Rome engendered a greater dependancy of each generation on the Classical world, its buildings, artefacts, and manners transposed in England to houses, furniture, decoration and the massing of a great Classical collection.

The 18th century was the period of the 'Collector'. Great houses were being built which conferred a very obvious and instantly recognisable status upon the owner. It became 'de rigeur' for the sons of the nobility to return from the Grand Tour with substantial proof that they had visited the right places, made friends with the right people and acquired the right knowledge. These 'proofs' included items of Italy's Classical past, marbles, coins, sculptures, bronzes, earthenware; items which conferred instant status on the owner. Batoni, an Italian artist specialising in portraiture and patronised by the English abroad, was frequently commissioned to paint the scion of a noble house in front of his trophies; when these trophies reached England they formed the basis of a collection.

Horace Walpole set out on his Grand Tour in 1739 with his friend Thomas Gray. He went to be fashionable, with letters of introduction to leaders of society in the cities in which he stayed; but his Tour was not strictly conventional – he was twenty two years old when he set off, without a tutor or bear leader, his character already well formed. From contemporary letters and those he wrote after the Grand Tour it appears that several things arising from it affected his later life: the friends he made, the spectacular scenery of the Alps, the discovery of Herculaneum and the antiquities he saw everywhere and which he brought back. Many of these antiquities remained housed in Arlington Street although Strawberry became the centre of a Collection which was diverse. Walpole seems to have collected everything that came his way, this included the conventional Roman copies of the Apollo Belvedere and the Farnese Flora, a bust of Caligula with silver eyes, coins, medals, miniatures, 12,000 prints of "English Heads" (the 18th century equivalent of the photograph), paintings, porcelain and bizarre items such as a Grinling Gibbons carved cravat in limewood, two dates preserved in an alabaster box and found in Herculaneum, locks of hair and beard cut from the head of Edward IV when his tomb was opened in 1789, the death warrant of Charles I and a copy of Magna Charta. He carefully scanned auction notices to see what would be on offer from other collectors, but with only one exception it does not seem to have included the natural items which were generally much sought after at the time – fossils and minerals: the exception was a cabinet full of shells housed in Arlington Street not Strawberry.

As the collection grew in size so the metamorphosis of Chopp'd Straw Hall into Strawberry Castle continued with an emphasis on collectable items which imparted a Gothic flavour.

The next extract is interesting for two reasons: firstly, it shows that by October of 1750 he had finally decided on battlements and was planning the changes of Strawberry into a castle, for him an essential element of Gothick, another being the cloister, and secondly, it shows that heraldry, genealogy and the glory of past family achievement had assumed a great significance for him.

It was through heraldry that Walpole set out to establish in his house a sense of theatre and the greatness of a period when knights rode out to fight the Saracen and to die for Christ in the Crusades. One of the principal ways in which it was used to promote this image at Strawberry was through the painted glass which he described as showing the "achievements of the old counts of Strawberry".

Walpole had visited a friend, Richard Bateman of Old Windsor, and there he found windows of Flemish glass which he thought would create the atmosphere he wanted for his house. This glass had been unearthed by an Italian, Asciotti, who had a Flemish wife; Walpole commissioned Asciotti to go to Flanders and find more of the glass for Strawberry. The result, for which he paid 36 guineas inclusive of Asciotti's expenses, was 450 pieces of glass, Flemish roundels. The subjects depicted were often taken from Biblical sequences, each sequence made up of several pieces of glass which together told a religious story, there were also pieces in grisaille showing drinking scenes, pedlars, pieces depicting birds and flowers and some glass with coats of arms. The majority of this glass was 16th century and early 17th century, stained in yellow and black with tonal variations achieved by mixing iron oxide together with silver nitrate, wine, urine and gum arabic. The later pieces were decorated in coloured enamels.

"To Sir Horace Mann,   Arlington Street, 18 October 1750
..... my castle will I believe begin to rear its battlements next spring. I have got an immense cargo of painted glass from Flanders: indeed several of the pieces are Flemish arms; but I call them the achievements of the old Counts of Strawberry. Adieu!"

His father, Robert Walpole, had become the most powerful man in the country when leading the government of George I, a king who didn't speak English, and who relied totally upon Robert, making him the first, or prime, minister. Robert was one of a line of land owning Norfolk squires, not a member of the great nobility or initially having great wealth. This lack of a noble background may be one of the reasons why Horace developed such an interest in lineage and ancestry; there were probably other reasons as well.

Various biographers have questioned whether Horace was actually the son of Robert Walpole. Robert and his wife Catherine Shorter were known to have led separate lives and there was a long gap between the births of Horace and their other children. Robert had openly taken a mistress, Maria Skerrett, whom he married after the death of Catherine. Horace was also totally dissimilar in face, build and pursuits to the immediate Walpole family, and it is fairly easy to understand why the supposition was raised that Horace might have had another father. Carr, Lord Hervey, was suggested. However, these questions on his ancestry appear to have been raised after his death and no contemporary comment is recorded. Lady Louisa Stuart, born forty years later than Horace, questioned the rumour, concluding that even if it were true she thought Horace certainly believed himself to be a Walpole. W. S. Lewis, the most committed Walpolian scholar, pointed out that Horace, although totally dissimilar to Robert Walpole and to his brothers, nevertheless bore a great resemblance to minor members of the family; I would suggest that there is a strong facial similarity to Galfridus Walpole. Lewis also noted that the Walpole men acted as godparents to Horace and argues that this makes it unlikely that Robert was not his father. In his early years Horace was very close to his mother, possibly too close, and it was only after her death that he became openly defensive of his father's political policy and attached himself to the Walpole men and Walpole genealogy. Whatever the truth of his birth Horace was certainly unlike the Walpole family in temperament and was further divided from his brothers by an age gap, this may provide another reason why he wanted to surround himself with coats of arms; delving back into the past may have given him a greater feeling of family unity and security.

❖❖❖

In the meantime he was kept busy by the death of Sir Hans Sloane, a fellow collector, who had died leaving Walpole one of the trustees of a collection containing 50,000 books, 3,560 manuscripts and countless other objects. These became the core of the British Museum.

"To Sir Horace Mann,   Arlington Street, 14 February 1753
You will scarce guess how I employ my time, chiefly at present in the guardianship of embryos and cockleshells. Sir Hans Sloane is dead, and has made me one of the trustees to his museum, which is to be offered for twenty thousand pounds to the King ..... He valued it at fourscore thousand, and so would anybody who loves hippopotamuses, sharks with one ear, and spiders as big as geese! It is a rent charge to keep the foetuses in spirits!"

Walpole had started a building programme soon after moving in to Strawberry Hill, altering, turning round and building onto the tiny Chopp'd Straw Hall, but it was not until 1753/4 with the transformation of Hall and Staircase and the addition of a Great Parlour or Refectory opening off the Hall with a Library above, that Gothick firmly became established.

Walpole's Gothick was fundamentally asymmetric on the exterior with the interior details derived from printed source material rather than from actual Gothic buildings of the past. He and the other members of the Committee of Taste, studied plates of the canopied tombs and choir screens of the great Gothic cathedrals and abbeys of Northern Europe. They found illustrations in Sandford's 'History of the Kings of England', Dart's 'Westmonasterium' and other books owned by Walpole. The engravings in these books had been produced in black and white and without a scale being given, which caused problems for the Committee. They attempted to replicate the original design in different materials partly for the sake of economy, but had no firm idea of the colour, texture or size of the item in its actual setting. This led to anomalies and later distressed Walpole who prided himself upon accuracy and truth to the Gothic source which meant first being true to the engravings and second being true to the tombs themselves. The Committee used the engravings much as we use wallpaper sample books today or magazines showing interior house design.

✦ ✦ ✦

The glass of Strawberry Hill became one of the most important features of the house in establishing Walpole's atmosphere of 'Gloomth', the word he coined to describe his 18th century / medieval mixture of gloom and warmth. The light in a cathedral such as Rheims is of paramount importance in concept and achievement of the atmosphere; in order to realise this in Strawberry Hill, whilst still admitting enough light for domestic living, he chose to use a combination of plain glass below and painted glass roundels of nine inches or less in size above, set in a surround of fragments of stained glass which gave the dark rich patterning of light found in medieval buildings. In the majority of early rooms the walls were grey or stone coloured and would therefore have been lit up by the sun falling through the glass and playing on floor and walls. About two thirds of this glass remains today although most has been reset.

We know in some detail the position of the glass in the 18th century, the changes that took place in the settings and the repositioning of the glass in the mid 19th century, also the 20th century changes to the glass that remains; recent research has traced the present whereabouts of much of the 'missing' glass. The original placing of the roundels within the 18th century rooms seems to have been fairly arbitrary without much attempt being made to gather together glass which had obviously come from the same sequence, so that the parable of the

Prodigal Son, for example, was split between different rooms rather than all the roundels being placed together. However, the glass in the Great North Bed-chamber, painted specially for Walpole by the York glass painter William Peckitt, is in its original lead setting, and on that glass can still be seen hand written directions giving the exact position of each piece within the overall make up of the window, the subject of which is heraldic, but which otherwise appears to have no precise format. It could reasonably be argued therefore that the glass throughout the house was grouped or positioned by Walpole for its aesthetic qualities rather than for any sequential or other reason.

"To Sir Horace Mann,   Strawberry Hill, 27 April 1753
I have brought two of your letters hither to answer: in town there are so many idle people beside oneself, that one has not a minute's time: here I have whole evenings, after the labours of the day are ceased. Labours they are, I assure you; I have carpenters to direct, plasterers to hurry, papermen to scold, and glaziers to help: this last is my greatest pleasure: I have amassed such quantities of painted glass, that every window in my castle will be illuminated with it: the adjusting and disposing it is vast amusement. I thank you a thousand times for thinking of procuring me some Gothic remains from Rome; but I believe there is no such thing there; I scarce remember any morsel in the true taste of it in Italy. Indeed, my dear Sir, kind as you are about it, I perceive you have no idea what gothic is; you have lived too long amidst true taste, to understand venerable barbarism. You say, 'You suppose my garden is to be Gothic too'. That can't be; Gothic is merely archictecture; and as one has a satisfaction in imprinting the gloomth of abbeys and cathedrals on one's house, so one's garden, on the contrary, is to be nothing but 'riant', and the gaity of nature. I am greatly impatient for my altar, and so far from mistrusting its goodness, I only fear it will be too good to expose to the weather, as I intend it must be, in a recess in the garden. I was going to tell you that my house is so monas-tic, that I have a little hall decked with long saints in lean arched windows and with taper columns, which we call the Paraclete, in memory of Eloisa's cloister ....."

In the early stages of the building programme the Gothic atmosphere of the house was mainly achieved through an asymmetric exterior and the use of painted glass and chimney-pieces built to resemble tombs. He talked about the "Gloomth" which he increased by a lack of interior lighting and by the filtering of exterior light coming into the house, but his description of the rooms in which he lived give the impression that most of the house at this period was ablaze with colour. The dark atmosphere was theatrically set in the Hall which acted as a type of permanent set or backdrop against which other scenes of life in the house could each be set within its coloured background.

A fragment of the Hall paper discussed in the following letter, supposedly painted by Bentley and a 'paperstainer' named Tudor, remains at Strawberry Hill. In his printed *Description* of the house of 1784 Walpole tells us that the source for the design on the paper was Prince Arthur's tomb in Worcester Cathedral. The fragment shows how very dark the paper was and therefore how dark the hall must have been; this is borne out by recent paint samples taken from the Hall Staircase. The scale seen in the fragment is odd; it does not appear to match the engraving of the Hall and Staircase published in the 1784 illustrated edition of the *Description* or any of the known watercolours showing the Hall. We know that in 1791 Cornelius Dixon, a Norfolk tradesman, was brought to Strawberry retouch the Hall paper and it is likely that the paper which remains in the house is his. He would therefore have repainted, rather than just retouched, the Hall, scaling down the design, which would have given a darker overall finish. This would make sense because in the period between the painting sessions, in September 1753, Walpole saw the Tomb itself and wrote to Bentley that he was surprised that it was built of stone, which had not been apparent from the engraving used as a source and which he had thought depicted a brass tomb. The darker, more perspectival look might well have been a deliberate attempt by Cornelius Dixon, working to Walpole's instruction, to more closely replicate the tomb.

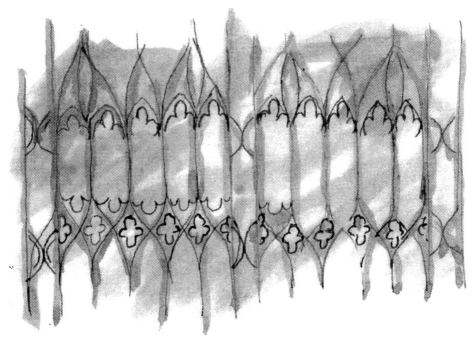

The overall effect produced by the Hall's painted tracery paper was to marry exterior and interior of the house. A new entrance was completed on the North side by 1759 and from then on Walpole's visitors would have arrived at a main entrance planned to resemble a medieval castle with battlements and the suggestions of a drawbridge, moat and dungeons, then they would have passed through the gate into an area of medieval cloister, complete with an oratory, a so called Prior's screen designed from a tomb in old St. Paul's cathedral, and a miniature Cloister, then on into the Hall of the house which had become the third element of Gothic, the Baronial Hall. The realistic trompe l'oeil painting of the walls, the illusion of a stone staircase, built of wood, replicating the library stair at Rouen Cathedral, the use of greys to increase the atmosphere and decrease the light, the placing of only one candle to illuminate the area: all these would have helped to achieve the atmosphere he wanted to create for visitors entering into the public space of the house. It is also possible to speculate that this extensive use of trompe l'oeil to produce a theatre of mood was inspired by Genoa, a city with palaces containing much trompe l'oeil work, which he visited on the Grand Tour.

❖ ❖ ❖

Wallpaper was still fairly new to the 18th century and Walpole seemed fascinated by it, the effect it could achieve, and the theatricality that it enhanced. He had one of the earliest print rooms described in the letter of 12 June 1753, (the effect produced in the room may be seen at the Jeremiah Lee Mansion, Marblehead, New England). He followed 18th century fashion in having papers which imitated different finishes or textures; in the description of his Great Parlour, or Eating Room, one of the earliest rooms finished in 1754, we are told that the walls were painted to imitate stucco. The height of that room is enhanced by the use of a very low dado rail thereby increasing the area of stucco which would have given a more theatrical, Gothic atmosphere, to the room.

During 20th century restoration a second piece of 18th century wallpaper was found together with a section of border, this paper looks like the Dutch delft tile paper described below as coming from his "cool little hall" and it has even been given printed crazing on the 'tiles', however it was found in a quite different area of the house on the second floor. In the 18th century one method of hanging paper was just that: to 'hang' it, as a tapestry would have been hung. It would have been tacked at the top to a batten, and would have hung freely down the wall, thereby absorbing bumps in the wall, before being secured at the base; it was therefore moveable. It is possible that the Dutch delft tile paper was repositioned to a bedchamber, possibly for a servant's use, or put into a second floor passage at a time when Walpole wanted to change the theme of the cool little Hall which he later converted into a Waiting Room for his visitors.

The 18th century and early 19th century free falling method of hanging wall-paper can still be seen in the Refectory, the Great North Bedchamber and the Beauclerc Tower of Strawberry Hill, where it is backed by hessian which would have helped to keep out the damp.

In building and cleaning work carried out in the 1980s to the room which he describes as the one in which they always lived (later his Blue Breakfast Room), it was found that the walls behind the paper were partly formed of 18th century tea chests. Walpole built as cheaply as possible only spending money on items for his Collection.

"To George Montagu,   Strawberry Hill, 11 June 1753
You will think me very fickle, and that I have but slight regard to the castle (I am building) of my ancestors, when you hear that I have been these last eight days in London amid dust and stinks, instead of syringa, roses, battlements and niches; .....

You may be assured that I will pay you a visit sometime this summer, though not yet, as I cannot leave my workmen, especially as we have a painter who paints the paper on the staircase under Mr. Bentley's direction. The armoury bespeaks the ancient chivalry of the lords of the castle, and I have filled Mr. Bentley's Gothic lanthorn with painted glass, which casts the most venerable gloom on the stairs that was ever seen since the days of Aberlard. The lanthorn itself in which I have stuck a coat of the Veres is supposed to have come from Castle Henningham ....."

"To Sir Horace Mann,   Strawberry Hill, 12 June 1753

I could not rest any longer with the thought of your having no idea of a place of which you hear so much, and therefore desired Mr. Bentley to draw you as much idea of it as the post would be persuaded to carry from Twickenham to Florence. The enclosed enchanted little landscape, then, is Strawberry Hill; and I will try to explain so much of it to you as will help to let you know whereabouts we are when we are talking to you; for it is uncomfortable in so intimate a correspondence as ours not to be exactly master of every spot where one another is writing, or reading, or sauntering. This view of the castle is what I have just finished, and is the only side that will be at all regular. Directly before it is an open grove, through which you see a field, which is bounded by a serpentine wood of all kind of trees, and flowering shrubs, and flowers. The lawn before the house is situated on the top of a small hill, from whence to the left you see the town and church of Twickenham encircling a turn of the river, that looks exactly like a seaport in minature.

The opposite shore is a most delicious meadow, bounded by Richmond Hill, which loses itself in the noble woods of the park to the end of the prospect on the right, where is another turn of the river, and the suburbs of Kingston as luckily placed as Twickenham is on the left: and a natural terrace on the brow of my hill, with meadows of my own down to the river, commands both extremities. Is not this a tolerable prospect? You must figure that all this is perpetually enlivened by a navigation of boats and barges, and by a road below my terrace, with coaches, post-chaises, waggons, and horsemen constantly in motion, and the fields speckled with cows, horses, and sheep. Now you shall walk into the house. The bow-window below leads into a little parlour hung with a stone-colour Gothic paper and Jackson's Venetian prints, which I could never endure while they pretended, infamous as they are, to be after Titian, etc., but when I gave them this air of barbarous bas-reliefs, they succeeded to a miracle: it is impossible at first sight not to conclude that they contain the history of Attila or Tottila, done about the very era. From hence, under two gloomy arches, you come to the hall and staircase, which it is impossible to describe to you as it is the most particular and chief beauty of the castle. Imagine the walls covered with (I call it paper, but it is really paper painted in perspective to represent) Gothic fretwork: the lightest Gothic balustrade to the staircase, adorned with antelopes (our supporters) bearing shields; lean windows fattened with rich saints in painted glass, and a vestibule open with three arches on the landing place, and niches full of trophies of old coats of mail, Indian shields made of rhinoceros's hides, broadswords, quivers, long bows, arrows, and spears – all supposed to be taken by Sir Terry Robsart in the holy wars. But as none of this regards the enclosed drawing, I will pass to that. The room on the ground-floor nearest to you is a bedchamber, hung with yellow paper and prints, framed in a new manner, invented by Lord Cardigan; that is, with black and white borders printed. Over this is Mr. Chute's bedchamber, hung with red in the same manner. The bow-window room [up] one pair of stairs is not yet finished; but in the tower beyond it is the charming closet where I am now writing to you. It is hung with green paper and water-colour pictures; has two windows; the one in the drawing looks to the garden, the other to the beautiful prospect; and the top of each glutted with the richest painted glass of the arms of England, crimson roses, and twenty other pieces of green, purple, and historic bits. I must tell you, by the way, that the castle, when finished, will have two-and-thirty windows enriched with painted glass. In this closet, which is Mr. Chute's College of Arms, are two presses with books of heraldry and antiquities, Madame Sévigné's letters, and any French books that relate to her and her aquaintance. Out of this closet is the room where we always live, hung with a blue and white paper in stripes adorned with festoons, and a thousand plump chairs, couches, and luxurious settees covered with linen of the same pattern, and with a bow-window commanding the prospect, and gloomed with limes that shade half each window, already darkened with painted glass in chiaroscuro, set in deep blue glass. Under this room is a cool little hall, where we generally dine, hung with paper to imitate Dutch tiles.

I have described so much, that you will begin to think that all the accounts I used to give you of the diminu-tiveness of our habitation were fabulous; but it is really incredible how small most of the rooms are. The only two good chambers I shall have are not yet built: they will be an eating-room and a library, each twenty by thirty, and the latter fifteen feet high. For the rest of the house, I could send it to you in this letter, only that I should have nowhere to live till the return of the post ....."

In the following letter he comments on the work of Sanderson Miller who was already established as a builder of Gothic houses and of Price who was brought in later to add colour to early grisaille glass in the Tribune.

"To Richard Bentley,   Arlington Street, September 1753
My dear Sir,
I am going to send you another volume of my travels; ..... I have made my visit at Hagley as I intended .....

As I got into Worcestershire, I opened upon a landscape of country which I prefer even to Kent, which I had reckoned the most beautiful county in England: but this, with all the richness of Kent, is bounded with mountains. Sir George Lyttelton's house is immeasurably bad and old: one room at the top of the house, which was reckoned a conceit in those days, projects a vast way into the air .....

You might draw, but I can't describe the enchanting scenes of the park: it is a hill of three miles, but broke into all manner of beauty; such lawns, such wood, rills, cascades, and a thickness of verdure quite to the summit of the hill, and commanding such a vale of towns and meadows, and woods extending quite to the Black Mountain in Wales, that I quite forgot my favourite Thames! – Indeed, I prefer nothing to Hagley but Mount Edgecumbe. There is extreme taste in the park: the seats are not the best, but there is not one absurdity. There is a ruined castle, built by Miller, that would get him his freedom even of Strawberry: it has the true rust of the Barons' Wars. Then there is a scene of a small lake with cascades falling down such a Parnassus! with a circular temple on the distant eminence; and there is such a fairy dale, with more cascades gushing out of rocks! and there is a hermitage, so exactly like those in Sadeler's prints, on the brow of a shady mountain, stealing peeps into the glorious world below! and there is such a pretty well under a wood, like the Samaritan woman's in a picture of Nicolo Poussin! and there is such a wood without the park, enjoying such a prospect! and there is such a mountain on t'other side of the park commanding all prospects, that I wore out my eyes with gazing, my feet with climbing, and my tongue and my vocabulary with commending! The best notion I can give you of the satisfaction I showed, was, that Sir George proposed to carry me to dine with my Lord Foley; and when I showed reluctance, he said, 'Why, I thought you did not mind any strangers, if you were to see anything!' Think of my not minding strangers! I mind them so much, that I missed seeing Hartlebury Castle, and the Bishop of Worcester's chapel of painted glass there, because it was his public day when I passed by his park. – Miller has built a Gothic house in the village at Hagley for a relation of Sir George: but there he is not more than Miller; in his castle he is almost Bentley .....

The cathedral is pretty, and has several tombs, and clusters of light pillars of Derbyshire marble, lately cleaned. Gothicism and the restoration of that architecture, and not of the bastard breed, spreads extremely in this part of the world. Prince Arthur's tomb, from whence we took the paper for the hall and staircase, to my great surprise, is on a less scale than the paper, and is not of brass but stone, and that wretchedly whitewashed. The niches are very small, and the long slips in the middle are divided every now and then with the trefoil .....

From Worcester I went to see Malvern Abbey. It is situated half way up an immense mountain of that name: the mountain is very long, in shape like the prints of a whale's back: towards the larger end lies the town. Nothing remains but a beautiful gateway and the church, which is very large: every window has been glutted with painted glass, of which much remains, but it did not answer: blue and red there is in abundance, and good faces; but the portraits are so high, I could not distinguish them. Besides, the woman who showed me the church would pester me with Christ and King David, when I was hunting for John of Gaunt and King Edward. The greatest curiosity, at least what I had never seen before, was, the whole floor and far up the sides of the church has been, if I may call it so, wainscoted with red and yellow tiles, extremely polished, and diversified with coats of arms, and inscriptions, and mosaic. I have since found the same at Glocester, and have even been so fortunate as to purchase from the sexton about a dozen, which think what an acquisition for Strawberry! They are made of the natural earth of the country, which is a rich red clay .....

The vale increases in riches to Glocester. I stayed two days at George Selwyn's house called Matson, which lies on Robin Hood's Hill: it is lofty enough for an Alp, yet is a mountain of turf to the very top, has wood scattered all over it, springs that long to be cascades in twenty places of it; and from the summit it beats even Sir G. Lyttelton's views, by having the city of Glocester at its foot, and the Severn widening to the horizon. His house is small, but neat. King Charles lay here at the siege; and the Duke of York, with typical fury, hacked and hewed the window-shutters of his chamber, as a memorandum of his being there. Here is a good picture of Dudley Earl of Leicester in his later age, which he gave to Sir Francis Walsingham, at whose house in Kent it remained till removed hither; and what makes it very curious, is, his age marked on it, 54 in 1572. I had never been able to discover before in what year he was born. And here is the very flower-pot and counterfeit association, for which Bishop Sprat was taken up, and the Duke of Marlborough sent to the Tower. The reservoirs on the hill supply the city. The late Mr. Selwyn governed the borough by them – and I believe by some wine too.

The Bishop's house is pretty, and restored to the Gothic by the last Bishop. Price has painted a large chapel window for him, which is scarce inferior for colours, and is a much better picture than any of the old glass. The eating-room is handsome. As I am a Protestant Goth, I was glad to worship Bishop Hooper's room, from whence he was led to the stake: but I could almost have been a Hun, and set fire to the front of the house, which is a small pert portico, like the conveniencies at the end of a London garden. The outside of the cathedral is beautifully light; the pillars in the nave outrageously plump and heavy. There is a tomb of one Abraham Blackleach, a great curiosity; for, though the figures of him and his wife are cumbent, they are very graceful, designed by Vandyck, and well executed. Kent designed the screen; but knew no more there than he did anywhere else how to enter into the true Gothic taste. Sir Christopher Wren, who built the tower of the great gateway at Christ Church, has catched the graces of it as happily as you could do: there is particularly a niche between two compartments of a window, that is a masterpiece.

But here is a modernity, which beats all antiquities for curiosity: Just by the high altar is a small pew hung with green damask, with curtains of the same; a small corner cupboard, painted, carved and gilt, for books, in one corner, and two troughs of a bird-cage, with seeds and water. If any mayoress on earth was small enough to enclose herself in this tabernacle, or abstemious enough to feed on rape and canary, I should have sworn that it was the shrine of the queen of the aldermen. It belongs to a Mrs. Cotton, who, having lost a favourite daughter, is convinced her soul is transmigrated into a robin-redbreast; for which reason she passes her life in making an aviary of the cathedral of Glocester. The chapter indulge this whim, as she contributes abundantly to glaze, whitewash and ornament the church.

King Edward's tomb is very light and in good repair. The old wooden figure of Robert, the Conqueror's unfortunate eldest son, is extremely genteel, and, though it may not be so ancient as his death, is in a taste very superior to anything of much later ages. Our Lady's Chapel has a very bold kind of portal, and several ceilings of chapels, and tribunes in a beautiful taste: but of all delight, is what they call the abbot's cloister. It is the very thing that you would build, when you had extracted all the quintessence of trefoils, arches, and lightness. In the church is a star-window of eight points, that is prettier than our rose windows ..... Adieu! my dear Sir!

Yours ever,

Hor. Walpole."

The tiles from "Glocester" cathedral were laid on the floor of the China Closet of Strawberry Hill; at this period the gothicising of the house was growing fast with the acquisition of arms and the setting of glass.

Mr. Palmer, engaged by Walpole to produce glass for Strawberry, worked in St. Martin's Lane, London, an area in which could be found many of the 18th century craftsmen employed at Strawberry Hill. Once Asciotti had determined there was a ready market for his Netherlandish and Flemish glass he worked with Palmer to produce ready-for-sale complete windows in painted glass, composed in sections of old glass and set within a framework of plain but highly coloured glass. These were too expensive for Walpole, who employed Palmer to create the same effect at Strawberry Hill for less money by adding a bright framework of stained glass to the Flemish pieces.

The Armoury mentioned below grew out of the three arched open Vestibule he had already described to Mann; it was on the landing of the house above the Hall.

"To Sir Horace Mann   Strawberry Hill, 6 October 1753
I fear the letter of July 21st which you tell me you have received, was the last I wrote. I will make no more excuses for my silence; I think they take up half my letters. The time of year must be full excuse; and this autumn is so dead a time, that people even don't die .....

I am totally ignorant, not to say indifferent about the Modenese treaty – indeed I have none of that spirit which was formerly so much objected to [by] some of my family, the love of negotiations, during a settled peace. Treaties within treaties are very dull businesses: contracts of marriage between baby-princes and miss-princesses give me no curiousity. If I had not seen it in the papers, I should never have known that master Tommy the archduke was playing at marrying Miss Modena – I am as sick of the hide and seek at which all Europe has been playing about a King of the Romans! Forgive me, my dear child, you who are a minister, for holding your important affairs so cheap. I amuse myself with Gothic and painted glass, and am as grave about my own trifles as I could be at Ratisbon. I shall tell you one or two events within my own very small sphere, and you must call them, a letter. I believe I mentioned having made a kind of armoury: my upper servant who is full as dull as his predecessor whom you knew, Tom Barney, has had his head so filled with arms, that t'other day when a man brought home an old chimney-back, which I had bought for having belonged to Harry VII, he came running in, and said, 'Sir, Sir! here is a man has brought some more armour!'

Last week when I was in town, I went to pay a bill to the glazier who fixed up the painted glass: I said, 'Mr. Palmer, you charge me seven shillings a day for your man's work; I know you give him but two shillings; and I am told that it is impossible for him to earn seven shillings a day' – 'Why no, Sir,' replied he, 'it is not that, but one must pay house rent, and one must eat – and one must wear' – I looked at him, and he had on, a blue silk waist-coat with an extremely broad gold lace – I could not help smiling. I turned round and saw his own portrait, and his wife's and his son's – 'And I see' said I, 'one must sit for one's picture: I am very sorry that I am to contribute for all you must do!' Adieu! I gave you warning that I had nothing to say."

*T*he Library at Strawberry Hill became Walpole's favourite room when it was finished and one of the strangest in the house; although Chute's designs, not Bentley's, were used for the Chimney-piece and the bookcases, Walpole and Bentley together designed the ceiling which was then painted by a Frenchman, Clermont. The theme shown on the ceiling was the crusades and the part played in them in defeating the infidel by Walpole's ancestors. This theme is picked up and repeated in a design above the bookcases of alternating catherine wheels and cross-crosslets. At one corner of the ceiling a Saracen's, or Moor's, head has been painted; this heraldic device and family crest was repeatedly used in the decoration of the house and symbolised the part played by the family, or the part Walpole claimed they had played, in the Crusades. In the Library it is presented as it was found on the tomb of Ludovic Robsart, Crusader knight and ancestor, with the catherine wheel above the bonnet of the Saracen, elsewhere in the house the wheel is placed on the bonnet.

This was the main library of Strawberry, housing part of Walpole's collection of about 7,200 books, not a particularly large number for the 18th century, nevertheless he never had enough space and books overflowed to other areas of house and grounds where he formed smaller libraries, including one placed in the Round Tower, and one in the grounds of the Little Cottage. It was a working library, with a catalogue compiled in 1763 by Walpole which Kirgate, who was also printer of the Strawberry Hill Press, kept updated. Each book was allotted a precise place in the presses around the room, each press, or case, housing a subject; for example: press A, to the right of the Chimney-piece housed works by Royal and Noble Authors: coins, medals and the fine arts were in B: fine arts continued in C: prints D: topography E: French literature (of which he owned 800 volumns) F and G: English history and literature H, I and K: the classics and Italian literature L and M: in addition to those letters each book had two numbers, allotted bottom to top and left to right of the press marks. A locked cabinet was added between presses D and E, in which were kept special books: a 2nd Folio Shakespeare, two esoteric editions dealing with the marking of swans' bills, some erotica and Alexander Pope's personal copy of Homer in which he had drawn Twickenham Church on the fly leaf and which Walpole greatly valued.

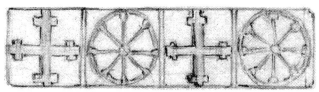

Po-Yang, in the following letter, was the name given to the goldfish pond in the garden of Strawberry Hill.

"To Richard Bentley,   Arlington Street, 19 December 1753
I little thought when I parted with you, my dear Sir, that your absence could indemnify me so well for itself; I still less expected that I should find you improving daily: but your letters grow more and more entertaining, your drawings more and more picturesque; you write with more wit, and paint with more melancholy, than ever anybody did: your woody mountains hang down somewhat so poetical, as Mr. Ashe said, that your own poet Gray will scarce keep tune with you. All this refers to your cascade scene and your letter. For the library, it cannot have the Strawberry imprimatur: the double arches and double pinnacles are most ungraceful; and the doors below the book-cases in Mr. Chute's design had a conventual look, which yours totally wants. For this time, we shall put your genius in commission, and, like some other regents, execute our own plan without minding our sovereign. For the chimney, I do not wonder you missed our instructions: we could not contrive to understand them ourselves; and therefore, determining nothing but to have the old picture stuck in a thicket of pinnacles, we left it to you to find out the how. I believe it will be a little difficult; but as I suppose facere quia impossibile est, is full as easy as credere, why – you must do it .....

The robber of Po-Yang is discovered, and I hope will be put to death, without my pity interfering, as it has done for Mr. Shorter's servant, or Lady Caroline Petersham's, as it did for Maclean. In short it was a heron. I like this better than thieves, as I believe the gang will be more easily destroyed, though not mentioned in the King's Speech or Fielding's treatises.

Lord Clarendon, Lord Thanet, and Lord Burlington, are dead. The second sent for his tailor, and asked him if he could make him a suit of mourning in eight hours: if he could, he would go into mourning for his brother Burlington – but that he did not expect to live twelve hours himself. Lord Burlington has left everything he had to his Countess for her life, then to Lady Hartington, and then to her son. The Marquis is not mentioned in the will. Can one doubt but he must have seen something in his son-in-law to merit such very marked omission? or can one more doubt that a capricious mother-in-law, an indulgent rich wife, and independent son, will find some opportunity to try all the candour of a Cavendish?

Yours ever,

H.W."

In the spring of 1754 Walpole wrote to John Chute from his town house advising him on the progress made to the new Eating Room where the builders had had a temporary lapse towards the Classical, and the Library at Strawberry; he was always careful with money and had persuaded Clermont to agree a fee for painting the library ceiling which cut the original quote almost in half. He continues the letter with a description of a visit of the Princess of Wales and her maid of honour, Elizabeth Chudleigh, to the opera.

"To John Chute,   Arlington Street, 30 April 1954
..... I have been forced to agree with Clermont for seventy pound. I have beat down fifty, but could not get it lower. The last time I went to Strawberry, I found the stucco men as busy as so many Irish bees, plastering up eggs and anchors for the frieze of the eating-room, but I soon made them destroy all they had done.

..... the only event since you left London was the tragi-comedy that was acted last Saturday at the opera. One of the dramatic guards fell flat on his face and motionless in an apoplectic fit. The Princess and her children were there. Miss Chudleigh, who 'apparemment' had never seen a man fall on his face before, went into the most theatric fit of kicking and shrieking that ever was seen. Several other women, who were preparing their fits, were so distanced, that she had the whole house to herself, and indeed such a confusion for half an hour I never saw! ....."

As the Hall, Staircase and Armoury grew more Gothic in appearance so the living areas of the house in which Walpole dined, sat and slept became prettier and more comfortable. The bow-window room discussed in the next letter is the Blue Bedchamber. Bromwich, a fashionable craftsman, employed paper stainers and plasterers who worked on the fabric of ceilings, chimney-pieces and screens throughout the house, together with a 'carver', possibly Murray, who was master carver and sculptor to the King and who was paid £8 by Walpole for work on the chimney-piece in the Little Parlour.

Portraits of Walpole, Gray, Williams and Bentley were painted in the Vandyke style by Eccardt.

"To Richard Bentley,   Arlington Street, 18 May 1754
My dear Sir,
Unless you will be exact in dating your letters, you will occasion me much confusion. Since the undated one which I mentioned in my last, I have received another as unregistered, with the fragment of the rock, telling me of one which has set sail on the 18th, I suppose of last month, and been driven back: this I conclude was the former. Yesterday, I received a longer, tipped with May 8th. You must submit to this lecture, and I hope will amend by it. I cannot promise that I shall

correct myself much in the intention I had of writing to you seldomer and shorter at this time of year. If you could be persuaded how insignificant I think all I do, how little important it is even to myself, you would not wonder that I have not much empressement to give the detail of it to anybody else. Little excursions to Strawberry, little parties to dine there, and many jaunts to hurry Bromwich, and the carver, and Clermont, are my material occupations. Think of sending these 'cross the sea! – The times produce nothing: there is neither party, nor controversy, nor gallantry, nor fashion, nor literature – the whole proceeds like farmers regulating them-selves, their business, their views, their diversions, by the almanac .....

The little that I believe you would care to know relating to the Strawberry annals, is, that the great tower is finished on the outside, and the whole whitened, and has a charming effect, especially as the verdure of this year is beyond what I have ever seen it: the grove nearest the house comes on much; you know I had almost despaired of its ever making a figure. The bow-window room, with a chintz bed and chairs; my father and mother over the chimney in the Gibbons frame, about which you know we were in dispute what to do. I have fixed on black and gold, and it has a charming effect over 'your chimney with the two dropping points', which is executed exactly; and the old grate of Henry VIII which you bought, is within it. In each panel round the room is a single picture; Gray's, Sir Charles Williams's, and yours, in their black and gold frames; mine is to match yours; and, on each side the door, are the pictures of Mr. Churchill and Lady Mary, with their son, on one side, Mr. Conway and Lady Ailesbury on the other. You can't imagine how new and pretty this furniture is. – I believe I must get you to send me an attestation under your hand that you knew nothing of it, that Mr. Rigby may allow that at least this one room was by my own direction. As the library and great parlour grow finished, you shall have exact notice."

Walpole was a Member of Parliament, rarely speaking in the House but aware of events happening around the world, and wanting to be involved behind the scenes in shaping policy. Most of the letters which weigh political comment are written to Mann. By 1754 Walpole was writing about the American War and here makes an early comment to Mann on George Washington.

"To Sir Horace Mann,   Arlington Street, 6 October 1754
You have the kindest way in the world, my dear Sir, of reproving my long silence, by accusing yourself. I have looked at my dates, and though I was conscious of not having written to you for a long time, I did not think it had

been so long as three months. I ought to make some excuse, and the truth is all I can make: if you have heard by any way in the world that a single event worth mentioning has happened in England for these three months, I will own myself guilty of abominable neglect. If there has not, as you know my unalterable affection for you, you will excuse me, and accuse the times. Can one repeat often, that everything stagnates? At present we begin to think that the world may be roused again, and that an East Indian war and a West Indian war may begat such a thing as an European war. In short, the French have taken such cavalier liberties with some of our forts, that are of great consequence to cover Virginia, Carolina, and Georgia, that we are actually despatching two regiments thither. As the climate and other American circumstances are against these poor men, I pity them, and think them too many, if the French mean nothing farther; too few, if they do. Indeed, I am one of those that feel less resentment when we are attacked so far off: I think it an obligation to be eaten the last.

You will have observed what precaution I had taken, in the smallness of the sheet, not to have too much paper to fill; and yet you see how much I have still upon my hands! As, I assure you, were I to fill the remainder, all I should say would be terribly wire-drawn, do excuse me: you shall hear an ample detail of the first Admiral Vernon that springs out of our American war; and I promise you at least half a brick of the first sample that is sent over of any new Porto Bello. The French have tied up the hands of an excellent fanfaron, a Major Washington, whom they took, and engaged not to serve for a year. In his letter, he said, 'Believe me, as the cannon-balls flew over my head, they made a most delightful sound.' When your relation, General Guise, was marching up to Cartagena and the Pelicans whistled round him, he said, 'What would Chloe give for some of these to make a pelican pie?' The conjecture made that scarce a rodomontade; but what pity it is, that a man who can deal in hyperboles at the mouth of a cannon, should be fond of them with a glass of wine in his hand! I have heard Guise affirm, that the colliers at Newcastle feed their children with fire-shovels! Good-night."

In November 1754 Walpole wrote a very tetchy letter to Bentley presumably in reply to an offer from Bentley to paint a Gothic design on the walls of the Little Parlour at Strawberry Hill. When the two men had envisaged the Hall replicating Arthur's tomb in Worcester Bentley had offered to paint it himself and Walpole had bought blank sheets of wallpaper from Bromwich awaiting Bentley's work; but Bentley had been dunned, had fled his creditors and gone to live in Jersey and Walpole had been forced to employ Tudor, an employee of Bromwich, to complete the painting.

"To Richard Bentley,   Arlington Street, 20 November 1754
..... now comes your last proposal about the Gothic paper. When you made
me fix up mine, unpainted, engaging to paint it yourself, and yet could never
be persuaded to paint a yard of it, till I was forced to give Bromwich's man
God knows what to do it, would you make me believe that you will paint a
room eighteen feet by fifteen?"

The letters to Richard Bentley are quite different in style from those written to
any of his other correspondents. One reason why Walpole is renowned as
possibly the greatest letter writer in the English language is for the variety of his
style and the letters to Bentley are quite remarkable.

Bentley's artistic style may be seen in the edition of Thomas Gray's poems
which he illustrated or in the chimney-pieces of Strawberry Hill. Each piece of
work is elegant, playful, full of beauty, allowing light to play a major part in
bringing the work to life. The drawings are rococo, highly ornamental and
display wit and insight. These facets of Bentley's character are also found in
Walpole's letters to him; they have an element of fun, joie de vivre and artistic
beauty conjuring up pictures that demonstrate the rapport between the two
men, and show what it was in Bentley that so delighted Walpole.

"To Richard Bentley,   Arlington Street, 6 March 1755
You know how late I used to rise: it is worse and worse: I stay late at debates
and committees; for, with all our tranquillity and my indifference, I think I am
never out of the House of Commons; from
thence, it is the fashion of the winter to go to vast
assemblies, which are followed by vast
suppers, and those by balls. Last week I
was from two at noon till ten at night at the
House; I came home, dined, new-dressed
myself entirely, went to a ball at Lord
Holdernesse's, and stayed till five in the morning.
What an abominable young creature! But why
may not I be so? Old Haslang dances at sixty-
five; my Lady Rochford without stays, and her
husband the new groom of the stole, dance.
In short, when Secretaries of State, Cabinet
Councillors, Foreign Ministers, dance like the
universal ballet in the Rehearsal, why should
not I – see them? In short, the true definition
of me is that I am a dancing senator – Not that
I do dance, or do anything by being a senator;

but I go to balls, and to the House of Commons – to look on; and you will believe me when I tell you, that I really think the former the more serious occupation of the two; at least the performers are most in earnest. What men say to women, is at least as sincere as what they say to their country."

Harry and Catherine in the following letter are two of Walpole's servants.

"To Richard Bentley,   Strawberry Hill, Wednesday, 11 June 1755
..... I was prevented from finishing my letter yesterday, by what do you think? By no less magnificent a circumstance than a deluge. We have had an extraordinary drought, no grass, no leaves, no flowers; not a white rose for the festival of yesterday! About four arrived such a flood, that we could not see out of the windows: the whole lawn was a lake, though situated on so high an Ararat: presently it broke through the leads, drowned the pretty blue bedchamber, passed through ceilings and floor into the little parlour, terrified Harry, and opened all Catherine's water-gates and speech-gates. I had but just time to collect two dogs, a couple of sheep, a pair of bantams, and a brace of gold fish; for, in the haste of my zeal to imitate my ancestor Noah, I forgot that fish would not easily be drowned. In short, if you chance to spy a little ark with pinnacles sailing towards Jersey, open the skylight, and you will find some of your acquaintance. You never saw such desolation!

A pigeon brings word that Mabland has fared still worse: it never came into my head before, that a rainbow-office for insuring against water might be very necessary. This is a true account of the late deluge.

Witness our hands,

Horace Noah.

Catherine Noah, her ✗ mark.

Henry Shem.

Louis Japhet.

Peter Ham, etc."

By 1755 the early building plan had been completed, the garden planted, and Walpole looked around for something new to interest him. In the same letter to Montagu in which he describes his farm, he sends a copy of a popular ballad circulating at the time, from which it is clear that Strawberry Hill was already well known and the subject of gossip. Almost all of the great houses mentioned in the ballad were either rebuilt or redesigned in the middle quarters of the 18th century.

"To George Montagu,   Strawberry Hill, 17 July 1755
Having done with building and planting, I have taken to farming; the first

fruits of my proficience in that science I offer to you, and have taken the liberty to send you a couple of cheeses. If you will give yourself the trouble to inquire at Brackley for the coach which set out this morning, you will receive a box and a roll of paper. The latter does not contain a cheese, only a receipt for making them ..... I have nothing more to send you but a new ballad which my Lord Bath has made on this place: you remember the old burden of it, and the last lines allude to Billy Bristow's having fallen in love with it.

1

Some talk of Gunnersbury,
For Sion some declare;
And some say that with Chiswick House
No villa can compare:
But all the beaux of Middlesex,
Who know the country well,
Say that Strawb'ry Hill, that Strawberry
Does bear away the bell.

2

Though Surry boast its Oatlands,
And Claremont kept so gim,
And though they talk of Southcote's,
It's but a dainty whim;
For ask the gallant Bristow,
Who does in taste excell,
If Strawb'ry Hill, if Strawberry
Don't bear away the bell.

I am a little pleased to send you this, to show you that in summer we are a little pretty, though you will never look at us but in our ugliness ....."

The old kitchen was turned into a China Closet where mainly everyday china was kept. The tiles from Glo[u]cester were laid on the floor carrying out the plan described in the letter of September 1753 to Richard Bentley. A new kitchen was eventually built at the base of the Round Tower in about 1760, but it remains a mystery where the kitchen was in the interim. It is possible that it was housed in one of the temporary wooden buildings to the west of the house, hidden in contemporary watercolours by clumps of trees – Walpole's favourite device for covering unsightly building materials, scaffolding and temporary buildings. For about forty years workmen, together with their materials, must have been present at Strawberry, but are never seen in paintings.

"To Richard Bentley,   Strawberry Hill, 31 October 1755
..... I have been thinning my wood of trees, and planting them out more into the field: I am fitting up the old kitchen for a china-room: I am building a bedchamber for myself over the old blue-room, in which I intend to die, though not yet; and some trifles of this kind, which I do not specify to you, because I intend to reserve a little to be quite new to you. Adieu!
        Yours ever,
                        Hor. Walpole"

The following letter to George Montagu gives a good idea of the type of garden and plants favoured by Walpole.

"To George Montagu,   Strawberry Hill, 8 November 1755
My Dear Sir
You oblige me extremely by giving me this commission, and though I am exceedingly unlike Solomon in everything else, I will at least resemble him, in recommending you to the Hiram from whom I obtained my cedars of

Libanus. He is by men called Christopher Gray, nurseryman at Fulham. I mention cedars first, because thay are the dearest; half a guinea apiece in baskets. The arbutus are scarce and a crown apiece, but they are very beautiful. The lignum vitae I would not recommend to you; they stink abominably if you touch them and never make a handsome tree: the Chinese arbor vitae is very beautiful. I have a small nursery myself, scarce bigger than one of those pleasant gardens which Solomon describes, and which if his fair one meant the church, I suppose must have meant the churchyard. Well, out of this little parsley-bed of mine, I can furnish you with a few plants, particularly three Chinese arbor vitaes; a dozen of the New England or Lord Weymouth's pine, which is that beautiful tree we have so much admired at the Duke of Argyle's for its clean straight stem, the lightness of its hairy green, and for being feathered quite to the ground: they should stand in a moist soil, and care must be taken every year to clear away all plants and trees round them, that they may have free air and room to expand themselves. Besides these I shall send you, twelve stone or Italian pines; twelve pinasters, twelve black spruce firs; two Carolina cherries; thirty evergreen cytisus, a pretty shrub that grows very fast, and may be cut down as you please; fifty Spanish brooms; and six acacias, the genteelist tree of all, but you must take care to plant them in a first row, and where they will be well sheltered, for the least wind tears and breaks them to pieces. All these are ready, whenever you will give me directions how and when to send them. They are exceedingly small, as I have but lately taken to propagate myself; but then they will travel more safely, will be more sure of living, and will grow faster than larger. Other sorts of evergreens that you must have, are silver and Scotch firs; Virginia cedars, which should stand forwards and have nothing touch them; and above all cypresses, which I think are my chief passion: there is nothing so picturesque when they stand two or three in a clump upon a little hillock or rising above low shrubs, and particularly near buildings. There is another bit of picture of which I am fond, and that is, a larch or a spruce fir planted behind a weeping willow, and shooting upwards as the willow depends. I think for courts about a house or winter gardens, almond trees mixed with evergreens, particularly with Scotch firs have a pretty effect, before anything else comes out; whereas almond trees, being generally planted among other trees, and being in bloom before other trees have leaves, and have no ground to show the beauty of their blossoms. Gray at Fulham sells cypresses in pots at half a crown apiece; you turn them out of the pot with all their mould and they never fail. I think this is all you mean; if you have any more garden questions or commissions, you know you command my little knowledge .....

Yours most sincerely

H.W."

A year later he wrote to Montagu again.

> "To George Montagu,   Strawberry Hill, October 14 1756
> ..... You bid me give some account of myself; I can in a very few words: I
> am quite alone; in the morning I view a new pond I am making for gold
> fish, and stick in a few shrubs or trees, wherever I can find a space, which
> is very rare: in the evening I scribble a little; all this mixed with reading; that
> is, I can't say I read much, but I pick up a good deal of reading. The only
> thing I have done that can compose a paragraph, and which I think you are
> Whig enough to forgive me, is, that on each side of my bed I have hung 'the
> magna charta', and the warrent for King Charles's execution, on which I
> have written 'major charta' as I believe without the latter the former by this
> time would be of very little importance ....."

The Little Cloister mentioned in the next letter is on the north side by the Main
Entrance to the house and close to the Front Door. In it stood Walpole's
goldfish 'tub' in which Selima the cat had drowned attempting to catch and eat
the fish swimming inside; she was later 'immortalised' – Gray's term – in his
'Ode on a Favourite Cat Drowned in a Tub of Goldfishes'. The poem was
written however without Gray being certain which one of the cats had actually
been drowned – Zara, Fatima or Selima. Oriental bowls at this time often had
painted interiors depicting weed, insects and fish; when filled with water the
fish and weed appeared to move and seemed very lifelike especially if a hand
was run across the surface to disturb the water. Walpole's 'tub' contained real
not painted fish. Is this perhaps an example of his sense of humour? Elsewhere
in Strawberry Hill the painted effects replaced the real, but at his Front Door
where guests waited to be admitted the illusion was found to be reality. It is
certain that he loved to amaze and surprise his guests.

❖ ❖ ❖

Henry VIII looms large on Walpole's royal horizon. He built a bedchamber
which he christened the Holbein Chamber to display portraits of the court of
Henry, collected an extraordinary clock given to Anne Boleyn by Henry, had
Tudor roses set into his windows, used the tomb of Henry's elder brother,
Arthur, as a source for the Hall and hung the dynastic portrait of Henry, which
now hangs at Sudeley Castle, in his own bedchamber. In his *Historic Doubts on
the Life and Reign of Richard III* he made the suggestion that Shakespeare's "The
Winter Evening's Tale" (The Winter's Tale) was built around the relationship
between Henry VIII and Anne Boleyn. He displayed less interest in the Stuarts.

The bed-chamber discussed below is The Holbein Chamber which has
always been one of the strangest rooms of the house. It was designed to be

seen in two sections; the bed itself standing divided from the remainder of the room by an ornate screen copied from one at Rouen cathedral, the central arch topped by Walpole's device of a Saracen's head with a catherine wheel and cross-crosslet surmounting the other two arches. The bed was covered in purple cut velvet, topped with "white and purple feathers on the centre of the tester", and copied for him from one at Burghley after he tried unsuccessfully to buy the genuine Burghley bed. It is shown in room plans and watercolours in different positions, but always close to the door, although it would have been more convenient if placed away from the door. The walls of both halves of the room were purple, and part of the first paper still exists; it was hung with some original Holbein drawings, and traced copies on oil-paper, said by Walpole to have been made "by Vertue from the original drawings of Holbein in queen Caroline's closet at Kensington, now removed to Buckingham house". The room was dominated by a chimney-piece partly modelled on Archbishop Wareham's tomb at Canterbury, he was the subject of one of the greatest of Holbein's drawings. The drawings were displayed in heavy black and gold ebonised frames which echoed Walpole's taste for japanned furniture, and ebony furniture from Goa. In this room it can be seen that he positioned certain objects for their atmosphere, appearance and associations and was ready to accept copies rather than have an alternative. To own the genuine object was not always imperative.

The construction of the Holbein Chamber marks a change in Walpole's design of the house: the alterations to Chopp'd Straw Hall were made to give a comfortable living space, but the Collection grew at an alarming rate and his later rooms were built to accommodate and display it. The Holbein Chamber is the first of these purpose built rooms.

✦ ✦ ✦

Müntz was the artist employed by Walpole and mentioned in the following letter to Horace Mann.

"To Sir Horace Mann,   Strawberry Hill, 9 September 1758
..... I am again got into the hands of builders, though this time to a very small extent; only the addition of a little cloister and bed-chamber. A day may come that will produce a gallery, a round tower, a larger cloister, and a cabinet, in the manner of a little chapel: but I am too poor for these ambitious designs yet, and I have so many ways of dispersing my money, that I don't know when I

shall be richer. However, I amuse myself infinitely; besides my printing-house, which is constantly at work, besides such a treasure of taste and drawing as my friend Mr. Bentley, I have a painter in the house, who is an engraver too, a mechanic, and everything. He was a Swiss engineer in the French service; but his regiment being broken at the peace, Mr. Bentley found him in the isle of Jersey and fixed him with me. He has an astonishing genius for landscape, and added to that, all the industry and patience of a German ..... In short, to finish all the works I have in hand, and all the schemes I have in my head, I cannot afford to live less than fifty years more ....."

Although Horace Walpole never married there are many comments in his letters that show how much he enjoyed the company of women and appreciated their beauty. The Duchesses of Hamilton and Richmond and Lady Ailesbury, who was married to Walpole's cousin Conway, were all renowned for their beauty and the shell seat in which they sat, mentioned in the letter below, was also famous for its beauty. It was a rococo bench which appeared to grow out of an oak tree, and had been designed by Bentley to stand in the garden close by a 'Gothic gate'.

"To George Montagu,   [Probably from Strawberry Hill] on 2 June 1759
Strawberry Hill is grown a perfect Paphos; it is the land of beauties. On Wednes-day the Duchesses of Hamilton and Richmond, and Lady Ailesbury dined there; the two latter stayed all night. There never was so pretty a sight as to see them all three sitting in the shell; a thousand years hence, when I begin to grow old, if that can ever be, I shall talk of that event, and tell young people how much handsomer the women of my time were than they will be then: I shall say, 'Women alter now' ..... Loo is mounted to its zenith; the parties last till one and two in the morning. We played at lady Hertford's last week, the last night of her lying-in, till deep into Sunday morning, after she and her lord were retired. It is now adjourned to Mrs. Fitzroy's ..... I proposed, that instead of receiving cards for assemblies, one should send in a morning to Dr. Hunter's, the man-midwife, to know where there is loo that evening ....."

The following two letters introduce the start of the next building phase. The bedchamber was eventually completed more than ten years later as a drawing room, designed by Robert Adam.

"To Horace Mann,   Strawberry Hill, 24 May 1760
..... The Parliament is up, and news are gone out of town; I expect none but what we receive from Germany. As to the Pretender, his life or death makes no impression here. When a real King is so soon forgot, how should an imaginary one be remembered? Besides, since Jacobites have found the way to St James's it is grown so much the fashion to worship kings, that people don't send their adorations so far as Rome. He at Kensington is likely long to outlast his old rival – The spring is far from warm, yet he wears a silk coat and has left off fires.

Thank you for the entertaining history of the Pope and the Genoese. I am flounced again into building – a round tower, gallery, cloister, and chapel, all starting up – if I am forced to run away by ruining myself, I will come to Florence, steal your nephew and bring him with me. Adieu!"

"To Horace Mann,   Arlington Street, 7 July 1760
.....I shall some time hence trouble you for some patterns of brocadella of two or three colours: it is to furnish a round tower that I am adding, with a gallery, to my castle: the quantity I shall want will be pretty large; it is to be a bedchamber entirely hung, bed and eight arm-chairs; the dimensions thirteen feet high, and twenty-two diameter. Your Bianca Capella is to be over the chimney. I shall scarce be ready to hang it these two years, because I move gently, and never begin till I have the money ready to pay, which don't come very fast, as it is always to be saved out of my income, subject too to twenty other whims and expenses. I only mention it now that you may at your leisure look me out half a dozen patterns; and be so good as to let me know the prices..... "

Ten years after arriving at Strawberry Hill Walpole started up his own private printing press, making him independent of publishers. It printed 34 books and a number of "detached pieces" and verses written to mark special occasions over a 32 year period. Most of the books were given to his friends as gifts, some were sold by Dodsley, the London publisher, who published the magnificent edition of Gray's poems illustrated by Richard Bentley. Kirgate was the longest serving of Walpole's printers arriving in 1765 and eventually becoming secretary and librarian as well as printer. It was to him that Walpole gave responsibility for cataloguing the prints in his Collection. The choice of what should be printed and the size of the print run was always made by Walpole, but decisions on typeface, paper etc. didn't interest him and were left to others. The press was associated in his mind with pleasure and his controversial political pamphlets were printed in London. Today the books from the Strawberry Hill Press are much sought after.

❖ ❖ ❖

The next three letters, the first from Strawberry Hill and the following two from his London home in Arlington Street, form a sequence and together reflect the great change brought about by the death of George II and the accession of George III. They start with an account of Walpole working on his book, *Anecdotes of Painting in England; with some Account of the Principal Artists and incidental Notes on the other Arts; collected by the late Mr. George Vertue; and now digested and published from his original MSS. by Mr. Horace Walpole.* This was written with great speed, became a success, and remains one of his best known literary works. It was published by the Strawberry Hill Press in 1762 with the first two volumes advertised for sale at 30 shillings. Walpole had bought the 39 workbooks containing Vertue's notes, meticulously kept throughout his life, of the great picture collections in stately houses around the country and their sale from one owner to the next. Vertue was one of the best of the 18th century engravers working on plates of treasures within these houses, including Houghton, Walpole's family home. Walpole said that he regarded the saving of Vertue's workbooks and the publication of the *Anecdotes* as his most useful work. He produced the first volume whilst chairbound with gout, it took him only eight months to write; the second was completed between 5th September and 23rd October. Four volumes were eventually published together with a *Catalogue of Engravers*, making five in all. Walpole's *Anecdotes* record the material which was later used as a foundation for the study of English art.

In the third letter of the following sequence, written to Montagu on 13th November, it is the theatricality of the Abbey which best pleased Walpole and the scene he described is very similar to one he used later in *The Castle of Otranto*.

"To George Montagu,   Strawberry Hill, 14 October 1760

If you should see in the newspapers, that I have offered to raise a regiment at Twickenham, am going with the expedition, and have actually kissed hands, don't believe it; though I own, the two first would not be more surprising than the last. I will tell you how the calamity befel me, though you will laugh instead of pitying me. Last Friday morning, I was very tranquilly writing my *Anecdotes of Painting* – I heard the bell at the gate ring – I called out, as usual, "Not at home;" but Harry, who thought it would be treason to tell a lie, when he saw red liveries, owned I was, and came running up: 'Sir, the Prince of Wales is at the door, and says he is come on purpose to make you a visit!' There was I, in the utmost confusion, undressed, in my slippers, and with my hair about my ears; there was no help, insanum vatem aspiciet – I went to receive him. Him was the Duke of York. Behold my breeding of the old Court; at the foot of the stairs I kneeled down, and kissed his hand. I beg your uncle Algernon Sidney's pardon, but I could not let the second Prince of the blood kiss my hand first. He was, as he always is, extremely good-humoured; and I, as I am not always, extremely respectful. He stayed two hours, nobody with him but Morrison; I showed him all my castle, the pictures of the Pretender's sons, and that type of the Reformation, Harry the Eight's measure, moulded into a weight to the clock he gave Anne Boleyn. But observe my luck; he would have the sanctum sanctorum in the library opened: about a month ago I removed the MSS. in another place. All this is very well; but now for the consequences; what was I to do next? I have not been in a Court these ten years, consequently have never kissed hands in the next reign. Could I let a Duke of York visit me, and never go to thank him? I know, if I was a great poet, I might be so brutal, and tell the world in rhyme that rudeness is virtue; or, if I was a patriot, I might, after laughing at Kings and Princes for twenty years, catch at the first opening of favour and beg a place. In truth, I can do neither; yet I could not be shocking; I determined to go to Leicester-house, and comforted myself that it was not much less meritorious to go there for nothing, than to stay quite away; yet I believe I must make a pilgrimage to Saint Liberty of Geneva, before I am perfectly purified, especially as I am dipped even at St. James's. Lord Hertford, at my request, begged my Lady Yarmouth to get an order for my Lady Henry to go through the park, and the Countess said so many civil things about me and my suit, and granted it so expeditiously, that I shall be forced to visit her, even before she lives here next door to my Lady Suffolk. My servants are transported; Harry expects to see me first Minister, like my father, and reckons upon a place in the Custom-House. Louis, who drinks like a German, thinks himself qualified for a page of the back stairs – but these are not all my troubles. As I never dress in summer, I had nothing upon earth but a frock, unless I went in black, like a poet, and pretended that a cousin was dead, one of the muses. Then I was in panic lest I should call my Lord Bute, your Royal Highness. I was not indeed in much pain at the conjectures the Duke of Newcastle would make on such an apparition, even if he would suspect that a new opposition was on foot, and that I was to write some letters to the Whigs.

Well, but after all, do you know that my calamity has not befallen me yet? I could not determine to bounce over head and ears into the drawing-room at once, without one soul knowing why I came thither. I went to London on Saturday night, and Lord Hertford was to carry me the next morning; in the mean time I wrote to Morrison, explaining my gratitude to one brother, and my unacquaintance with t'other, and how afraid I was that it would be thought officious and forward if I was presented now, and begging he would advise me what to do; and all this upon my bended knee, as if Schutz had stood over me and dictated every syllable. The answer was by order from the Duke of York, that he smiled at my distress, wished to put me to no inconvenience, but desired, that as the acquaintance had begun without restraint, it might continue without ceremony. Now I was in more perplexity than ever! I could not go directly, and yet it was not fit it should be said I thought it an inconvenience to wait on the Prince of Wales. At present it is decided by a jury of court matrons, that is, courtiers, that I must write to my Lord Bute and explain the whole, and why I desire to come now

– don't fear: I will take care they shall understand how little I come for. In the mean time, you see it is my fault if I am not a favourite .....

P.S. If I had been told in June, that I should have the gout, and kiss hands before November, I don't think I should have given much credit to the prophet."

"To George Montagu,   Arlington street, 25 October 1760
                                  I tell a lie, I am at Mr. Chute's
Was ever so agreeable a man as King George the Second, to die the very day it was necessary to save me from ridicule? I was to have kissed hands to-morrow – but you will not care a farthing about that now; so I must tell you all I know of departed majesty. He went to bed well last night, rose at six this morning as usual, looked, I suppose, if all his money was in his purse, and called for his chocolate. A little after seven, he went into the water-closet; the German valet de chambre heard a noise louder than royal wind, listened, heard something like a groan, ran in, and found the hero of Oudenarde and Dettingen on the floor, with a gash on his right temple, by falling against the corner of a bureau – he tried to speak, could not, and expired. Princess Emily was called, found him dead, and wrote to the Prince. I know not a syllable, but am come to see and hear as much as I can. I fear you will cry and roar all night, but one could not keep it from you. For my part like a new courtier, I comfort myself, considering what a gracious Prince comes next. ....."

"To George Montagu,   Arlington Street, 13 November 1760
Even the honeymoon of a new reign don't produce events every day. There is nothing but the common saying of addresses and kissing hands .....

For the King himself, he seems all good-nature and wishing to satisfy everybody; all his speeches are obliging. I saw him again yesterday, and was surprised to find the levee-room had lost so entirely the air of the lion's den. This sovereign don't stand in one spot, with his eyes fixed royally on the ground, and dropping bits of German news; he walks about, and speaks to everybody. I saw him afterwards on the throne, where he is graceful and genteel, sits with dignity, and reads his answers to addresses well; .....

Do you know, I had the curiosity to go to the burying t'other night; I had never seen a royal funeral; I walked as a rag of quality, which I found would be, and so it was, the easiest way of seeing it. It is absolutely a noble sight. The Prince's Chamber, hung with purple, and a quantity of silver lamps, the coffin under a canopy of purple velvet, and six vast chandeliers of silver on high stands, had a very good effect ..... The procession, through a line of foot-guards, every seventh man bearing a torch, the horse-guards lining the outside, their officers with drawn sabres and crape sashes on horseback, the drums muffled, the fifes, bells tolling, and minute guns, – all this was very solumn. But the charm was the entrance of the Abbey, where we were received by the Dean and chapter in rich copes, the choir and alms-men all bearing torches; the whole Abbey so illuminated, that one saw it to greater advantage than by day; the tombs, long aisles, and fretted roof, all appearing distinctly, and with the happiest chiaro scuro. There wanted nothing but incense, and little chapels, here and there with priests saying mass for the repose of the defunct – yet one could not complain of its not being Catholic enough. I had been in dread of being coupled with some boy of ten years old – but the heralds were not very accurate, and I walked with George Grenville, taller and older enough to keep me in countenance. When we came to the chapel of Henry VII, all solemnity and decorum ceased – no order was observed, people sat or stood where they could or would, the yeomen of the guard were crying out for help, oppressed by the immense weight of the coffin; the Bishop read sadly, and blundered in the prayers; the fine chapter, Man that is born of a woman, was chanted not read, and the anthem, besides being unmeasurably tedious, would have served as well for a nuptial. The real serious part was the figure of the Duke of Cumberland, heightened by a thousand melancholy circumstances. He had a dark brown adonis, and a cloak of black cloth with a train of five yards. Attending the funeral of a father how little reason soever he had to love him, could not be pleasant. His leg extremely bad, yet forced to stand upon it near two hours, his face bloated and distorted with his late paralytic stroke, which has affected too one of his eyes, and placed over the mouth of the vault, into which in all probability he must himself so soon descend – think how unpleasant a situation! He bore it all with a firm and unaffected countenance. This grave scene was fully contrasted by the burlesque Duke of Newcastle – he fell into a fit of crying the moment he came into the chapel, and flung himself back in a stall, the Archbishop hovering over him with a smelling-bottle – but in two minutes his curiosity got the better of his hypocrisy and he ran about the chapel with his glass to spy who was or was not there, spying with one hand, and mopping his eyes with t'other. Then returned the fear of catching cold, and the Duke of Cumberland, who was sinking with heat, felt himself weighed down, and turning round, found it was the Duke of Newcastle standing upon his train, to avoid the chill of the marble. It was very theatric to look down into the vault, where the coffin lay, attended by mourners with lights ....."

In the next letter purporting to have nothing to say, he 'throws away' the line "my castle is built of paper". Papier-mâché is one of the main building materials he used at Strawberry Hill for the great moulded ceilings and even for part of the walls themselves which, combined with lathe and plaster, were protected by an outer coating of render and an 18th century form of pebble dash. Papier-mâché was a popular and fashionable material in the 18th century, used for buildings – as in the Royal Pavilion at Brighton – for chairs and tables, and for ornament.

Papier-mâché was produced by wallpaper manufacturers wanting to make use of what might otherwise be a waste product. It is apparent from the number of times Walpole mentions the paper in a matter of fact way in his letters that he did not consider its use unusual, just thrifty: Strawberry Hill was not a great house, therefore it did not have to be constructed only of stone or brick. This use of papier-mâché must have increased Walpole's image of his house as a piece of theatre. Theatricality may also have been the purpose behind the choice of a "convolvuluse" painted ceiling which he mentions to Mann.

It is ironic, but gently pleasing, that he should be so wrong about the length of time the house would stand. 200 years after his death in 1797 and 300 from the first building of Chopp'd Straw Hall it stands as solidly as when he first wrote that he expected it to last for only ten years.

"To Horace Mann,   Arlington Street, 27 January 1761
I should like Marshal Botta's furniture that you describe if my tenure in Strawberry were as transitory as a Florentine commander's; but in a castle built for eternity and founded in the most flourishing age of the greatest republic now in the world, which has extended its empire into every quarter of the globe, can I think of a peach-coloured ground, which will fade like the bloom on Chloe's cheek? – there's a pompous paragraph! a Grecian or a Roman would have written it seriously, and with even more slender pretensions. However, though my Castle is built of paper, and though our empire should vanish as rapidly as it has advanced, I still object to peach-colour – not only for its fading hue, but for wanting the solemnity becoming a Gothic edifice: I must not have a round tower dressed in a pet-en-l'air. I would as soon put rouge and patches on a statue of St Ethelburgh. You must not wonder at my remembering Rinuncini's hangings at the distance of nineteen or twenty years; my memory is exceedingly retentive of trifles. There is no hurry; I can wait till you send me patterns, and an account of that triple-coloured contexture; for which, in gratitude to my memory, I still have a hankering. Three years ago I had the ceiling of my china room painted from one I had observed in the little Borghese Villa, I was hoarding ideas for a future Strawberry even in those days of giddiness, when I seemed to attend to nothing ....."

I have delivered to your brother the famous pamphlet, two sets of the *Royal and Noble* Authors for yourself and Lady Mary Wortley, a Lucan printed at Strawberry, which I trust you will think a handsome edition, and six of the newest-fashioned and prettiest fans I could find – they are really genteel, though one or two have caprices that will turn a Florentine head. They were so dear that I shall never tell you the price; I was glad to begin to pay some of the debts I owe you in commissions ....."

Walpole at this time was forty three and very slight. He was described by Laetitia Matilda Hawkins as being 'not merely tall, but more properly long and slender to excess' and as walking 'knees bent, and feet on tip toe, as if afraid of a wet floor'.

Henrietta Howard, Lady Suffolk, was his friend and neighbour at Marble Hill, a perfect Palladian villa built in the 1720s on the Thames, designed by Colen Campbell and Lord Pembroke and built by Roger Morris with the garden planned by Alexander Pope assisted by Bridgeman; it was therefore a very different house from Strawberry Hill. She was the long suffering mistress of George II, very deaf and much loved by society. Her niece, Henrietta Hotham, lived with her at Marble Hill and was a great favourite of Walpole; he spoke of her as "the little Hotham" and wrote for her *The Magpie and her Brood*.

"To Henry Seymour Conway,   Strawberry Hill, 5 August 1761
This is the 5th of August, and I just receive your letter of the 17th of last month by Fitzroy. I heard he had lost his pocket-book with all his dispatches, but had found it again. He was a long time finding the letter for me.

You do nothing but reproach me; I declare I will bear it no longer, though you should beat forty more marshals of France. I have already writ you two letters that would fully justify me if you receive them; if you do not, it is not I that am in fault for not writing, but the post offices for reading my letters, content if they would forward them when they have done with them. They seem to think, like you, that I know more news than anybody. What is to be known in the dead of summer, when all the world is dispersed? Would you know who won the sweepstakes at Huntington? What parties are at Woburn? What officers upon guard in Betty's fruit-shop? Whether the peeresses are to wear long or short tresses at the Coronation? How many jewels Lady [Harrington] borrows of actresses? All this is your light summer wear for conversation; and if my memory were as much stuffed with it as my ears, I might have sent you volumes last week. My nieces, Lady Waldegrave, and Mrs. Keppel, were here five days, and discussed the claim or disappointment of every miss in the kingdom for Maid of Honour. Unfortunately this new generation is not at all my affair. I cannot attend to what concerns them – Not that their trifles are less important than those of one's own time, but my mould has taken all its impressions, and can receive no more. I must grow old upon the stock I have. I, that was so impatient at all their chat, the moment they were gone, flew to my Lady Suffolk, and heard her talk with great satisfaction of the late Queen's Coronation petticoat. The preceding age always appears respectable to us (I mean as one advances in years), one's own age interesting, the coming age neither one nor t'other.

You may judge by this account that I have writ all my letters, or ought to have written them; and yet, for occasion to blame me, you draw a very pretty picture of my situation: all which tends to prove that I ought to write to you every day, whether I have anything to say or not. I am writing, I am building – both works that will outlast the memory of battles and heroes! Truly, I believe, the one will as much as t'other. My buildings are paper, like my writings, and both will be blown away in ten years after I am dead; if they had not the substantial use of amusing me while I live, they would be worth little indeed ....."

The following letter to Montagu is written before his friend left for Dublin. In the building scheme the Cabinet or Tribune was prefabricated and erected on site.

"To George Montagu,   Strawberry Hill, 20 August 1761
A few lines before you go. Your resolutions are good, and give me great pleasure; bring them back unbroken. I have no mind to lose you – we have been acquainted these thirty years, and to give the devil his due, in all that time, I never knew a bad, a false, a mean or ill-natured thing in the devil – but don't tell him I say so – especially as I cannot say the the same of myself. I am now doing a dirty thing, flattering you to preface a commission. Dicky Bateman has picked up a whole cloister-full of old chairs in Herefordshire – he bought them one and one, here and there in farm-houses, for three and sixpence and a crown apiece. They are of wood, the seats triangular, the backs, arms, and legs loaded with turnery. A thousand to one but there are plenty up and down Cheshire too – if Mr and Mrs Wetenhall, as they ride or drive out, would now and then put up such a chair, it would oblige me greatly. Take notice, no two need be of the same pattern .....

I am expecting Mr Chute to hold a chapter on the cabinet – a barge-load of niches, window-frames and ribs is arrived. The cloister is paving, the privy-garden making, painted glass adjusting to the windows on the back-stairs – with so many irons in the fire, you may imagine I have not much time to write. I wish you a safe and pleasant voyage.

Yours faithfully

H.W."

In the letter of 9th September Walpole is at his best, acting as social commentator.

"To Henry Seymour Conway,   Arlington Street, 9 September 1761
The date of my promise is now arrived, and I fulfil it – fulfil it with great
satisfaction, for the Queen is come; I have seen her, have been presented to
her – and may go back to Strawberry. For this fortnight I have lived upon the
road between Twickenham and London: I came, grew impatient, returned;
came again, still to no purpose. The yachts made the coast of Suffolk last
Saturday, on Sunday entered the road of Harwich, and on Monday morning
the King's chief eunuch, as the Tripoline ambassador calls Lord Anson, landed
the Princess. She lay that night at Lord Abercorn's at Witham, the palace of
silence; and yesterday at a quarter after three arrived at St. James's. In half an
hour one heard of nothing but proclamations of her beauty: everybody was
content, everybody pleased. At seven one went to court. The night was sultry.
About ten the procession began to move towards the chapel, and at eleven
they all came up into the drawing-room. She looks very sensible, cheerful,
and is remarkably genteel. Her tiara of diamonds was very pretty, her
stomacher sumptuous; her violet-velvet mantle and ermine so heavy, that the
spectators knew as much of her upper half as the King himself. You will have
no doubts of her sense by what I shall tell you. On the road they wanted her
to curl her toupet: she said she thought it looked as well as that of any of the
ladies sent to fetch her; if the King bid her, she would wear a periwig,
otherwise she would remain as she was. When she caught the first glimpse
of the Palace, she grew frightened and turned pale; the Duchess of Hamilton
smiled – the Princess said, 'My dear Duchess, you may laugh, you have been
married twice, but it is no joke to me.' Her lips trembled as the coach
stopped, but she jumped out with spirit, and has done nothing but with
good-humour and cheerfulness. She talks a great deal – is easy, civil, and not
disconcerted. At first, when the bridesmaids and the court were introduced
to her, she said, 'Mon Dieu, il y en a tant, il y en a tant!' She was
pleased when she was to kiss the peeresses; but Lady Augusta was
forced to take her hand and give it to those that were to kiss it,
which was prettily humble and good
natured. While they waited for supper, she
sat down, sung, and played. Her French is
tolerable, she exchanged much both of that and
German with the King, the Duke, and the Duke of
York. they did not get to bed till two. To-day was
a drawing-room: everybody was presented to
her; but she spoke to nobody, as she could
not know a soul. The crowd was much

less than at a birth-day, the magnificence very little more. The King looked very handsome, and talked to her continually with great good-humour. It does not promise as if they two would be the two most unhappy persons in England, from this event. The bridesmaids, especially Lady Caroline Russel, Lady Sarah Lenox, and Lady Elizabeth Keppel, were beautiful figures. With neither features nor air, Lady Sarah was by far the chief angel. The Duchess of Hamilton was almost in possession of her former beauty to-day; and your other Duchess, your daughter, was much better dressed than ever I saw her. Except a pretty Lady Sutherland, and a most perfect beauty, an Irish Miss Smith, I don't think the Queen saw much else to discourage her: my niece, Lady Kildare, Mrs. Fitzroy, were none of them there. There is a ball to-night, and two more drawing-rooms; but I have done with them. The Duchess of Queensbury and lady Westmoreland were in the procession, and did credit to the ancient nobility.

You don't presume to suppose, I hope, that we are thinking of you, and wars, and misfortunes, and distresses, in these festival times. Mr. Pitt himself would be mobbed if he talked of anything but clothes, and diamonds, and bridemaids. Oh! yes, we have wars, civil wars; there is a campaign opened in the Bed-chamber. Everybody is excluded but the ministers; even the Lords of the Bed-chamber, cabinet counsellors, and foreign ministers: but it has given such offence that I don't know whether Lord Huntingdon must not be the scape-goat. Adieu!"

The Gallery is the great room of the house and the Cabinet (also known as the Tribune or Chapel) possibly the most original room. There are several different ways of appreciating and understanding Strawberry Hill; one of these is to see it as purpose built to house an idiosyncratic collection – part of this being the chimney-pieces, screens, ceilings and painted walls. The Gallery and Cabinet, which must be considered an integral part of Walpole's Collection, fulfilled the function of display cases for special objects within the Collection. Once these rooms were finished Walpole resumed his travels instead of devoting most of his energy and time to acquiring yet more objects.

The Gallery, known as the Long Gallery, is 56 feet long, 17 feet high and 13 feet wide with added side recesses; it was built on the West side of the house immediately over an open Great Cloister. Several different sources were given for various areas of the Gallery: the glass gallery of Chantilly, Archbishop Bourchier's tomb at Canterbury, the North door of St. Albans. The magnificent ceiling made in papier-mâché was copied from a section of the side aisles of the Henry VII chapel at Westminster Abbey.

John Chute and Thomas Pitt (a close neighbour) designed the chimney-piece. Pitt was the first of the gentlemen architects 'employed' by Walpole who had travelled in Spain and appreciated Moorish architecture; this influence can be seen in the chimney and in the use of the gilded fretwork over glass which decorates the mirrored niches of the Gallery.

As an 18th century gallery it is unusual; standard practice had long plain windows interspersed with mirrors: paintings or tapestries would then be hung on the opposite walls. Walpole made a major change. He placed windows set with heraldic glass to run the length of the gallery, with family portraits hanging between them; he then placed his mirrored wall (necessary to reflect, increase and distribute light) facing the windows, not between them, and over the surface of the mirrors with their lattice work of gold fretwork he hung more family portraits. With walls of crimson Norwich damask, furniture of the same material framed in black and gold, gold fretworked mirrors, portraits filling every available space, and rare items from the collection carefully displayed, it must have been ablaze with colour. However, Thomas Gray, when he visited just described it as 'all gothicism and gold and crimson and looking glass'.

Walpole's friends would have reached the Long Gallery after coming through the gloomth of the Hall, maybe after dining in the Great Parlour which had stone coloured walls, and would have continued onwards passing the Armoury, which again was painted grey and would therefore have been another dark area. A premonition of the change they were about to encounter would have been given as they passed through the Star Chamber (an ante-room at the top of the stairs) painted or papered with pink walls and with one wall taken up by a window of painted glass. Two of the chairs in the Star Chamber were also brightly coloured in blue and white. The brilliant colours must have been breath-

taking after the darkness of the grey stone painted walls of the Hall and Armoury lit by only a single candle. Going onwards the visitor would have passed down a narrow corridor dimly illuminated by a small skylight window of painted glass, and presumably by only one candle as Walpole mentions only one candlestick, and they would have passed through this passageway into the Gallery. The effect must have been very theatrical. All the central walk-ways of the house were a preparation for the brilliance of Walpole's Gallery and in it, in a prominent position, he displayed one of his most precious possessions, an eagle which he describes as "found in the gardens of Boccapadugli within the precinct of Caracalla's baths at Rome, in the year 1742. One of the finest pieces of Greek sculpture in the world, and reckoned superior to the eagle in the villa Mattei." Also here were family portraits which he valued greatly, by Reynolds, Hudson and others. Here too hung some of the greatest paintings in the Collection including "a young man's head, aet 18; admirable nature: by Giorgione. This was in the collection of Charles I", and a Poussin. In the window stood bronzes of an Ibis, Ceres with a cow in her lap, and an ostrich, this last listed as "very spirited". It was rare for Walpole to collect artefacts representing animals, although he kept a large number of household pets at Strawberry and obviously had a great attachment to them all and particularly for his small King Charles spaniel dogs which are frequently mentioned in his letters.

❖ ❖ ❖

If the Gallery was a centre piece for the family portraits within the Collection, then the Cabinet or Tribune was the display area for his most precious items. The only way into it was from the Gallery through two Gothic tracery doors, resembling the entrance to a treasury vault. The inner door was fretted and at first glance it appeared to be a continuation of the Long Gallery mirrors and niches. The treasures could be glimpsed through it but not necessarily reached: another trompe l'oeil effect. It was a special room and only the most privileged were invited to enter. They would have left the blaze of colour in the Gallery for a dolls' house size tower-like room in which individual items shone out. A star window in the ceiling let in light through golden glass described as "shedding a golden gloom", and the remaining windows were filled with brightly painted glass – 16th century glass reworked by Price in the 18th century to make it brighter and more colourful and to exclude natural light. The Tribune is not in fact a tower, although with each corner modified and recessed it has the feel of one. It still retains a theatricality and charm with an air of being in the heart of the castle; it is immensely quiet, and it exudes an atmosphere which Walpole described as being like "a Catholic chapel". This was enhanced by the presence of a raised altar of black and gold standing to the right of the door, for which the tomb of two of the children of Edward III in Westminster Abbey was the source, on it a Florentine box inlaid with precious stones which had been given to Walpole by Horace Mann. Above this stood a rosewood cabinet, which can now be found in the Victoria and Albert Museum, originally designed to house enamels and miniatures, and decorated with bas-relief and ivory statues.

The Tribune, a very small room, about 16 feet across, was listed by Walpole in 1774 as containing 36 sculptures and statues, 92 miniatures and enamels, 77 paintings and drawings and 189 other treasures. It is very hard to imagine them all in the room and when John Carter painted a watercolour of the Tribune he made it appear much larger than in fact it is; his painting does not make it look overcrowded with treasures, but it must have been filled to overflowing.

I quote five entries from Walpole's *Description* of the Tribune to give some idea of how diverse was the Collection: (today, with hindsight, we know that his attributions were not always correct).

"Hair of king Edward IV cut from his corpse when discovered in St. George's chapel at Windsor, 1789; given by Sir Joseph Banks.

A small bust in bronze of a Caligula, with silver eyes. This exquisite piece is one of the finest things in the collection, and shows the great art of the ancients. It is evidently a portrait, carefully done, and seems to represent that emperor at the beginning of his madness. It was found with some other small busts at the very first discovery of Herculaneum, which happened by digging a well for the prince d'Elboeuf, who resided many years afterwards at Florence, where it was sold on his return to France, and, being purchased by Sir Horace Mann, was by him sent to Mr. Walpole.

A magnificent missal, with miniatures by Raphael and his scholars, set in gold enamelled, and adorned with rubies and turquoises; the sides are of cornelian, engraved with religious subjects; the clasp, a large garnet. This precious prayer-book belonged to Claude queen of France, wife of Francis I and seems to have belonged to the father of Thuanus; vide vol.1 p.142, of the French edition. It was purchased by Mr. Walpole from the collection of doctor Meade, 1755.

A point cravat carved by Gibbons; a present by Mr. Grosvenor Bedford.

A most beautiful silver bell, made for a pope by Benvenuto Cellini. It is covered all over in the highest relievo with antique masks, flies, grasshoppers, and other insects; the virgin and boy-angels at top, a wreath of leaves at bottom. Nothing can exceed the taste of the whole design, or the delicate and natural representation of the insects: the wonderful execution makes almost every thing credible that he says of himself in his Life. It came out of the collection of the Marquis of Leonati at Parma, and was bought by the Marquis of Rockingham, who exchanged it with Mr. Walpole for some very scarce Roman medals of great bronze, amongst which was an unique medaliuncino of Alexander Severus with the amphitheatre, in the highest preservation."

Today, when we read about this glittering Collection it is necessary to bear in mind that he had a strike of his workforce because they thought he was paying an insufficient wage. He said that he was building economically; in fact, his money was spent on the items within the collection not on the building of the house.

"To Sir Horace Mann,   Strawberry Hill, 1 July 1762
..... I am in distress about my Gallery and Cabinet: the latter was on the point of being completed, and is really striking beyond description. Last Saturday night my workmen took their leave, made their bow, and left me up to the knees in shavings. In short, the journeymen carpenters, like the cabinet-makers, have entered into an association not to work unless their wages are raised – and how can one complain? The poor fellows, whose all the labour is, see their masters advance their prices every day, and think it reasonable to touch their share. You would be frightened at the dearness of everything; I build out of economy, for unless I do now, in two years I shall not be able to afford it. I expect that a pint of milk will not be sold under a diamond, and then nobody can keep a cow but my Lord Clive ....."

The battlements, together with the pinnacles which gave the house the skyline of a castle were first built of wood and had to be replaced several times.

"To the Earl of Strafford,   Strawberry Hill, 5 August 1762
..... You tantalise me by talking of the verdure of Yorkshire; we have not had a teacup full of rain till to-day for these six weeks. Corn has been reaped that never wet its lips; not a blade of grass; the leaves yellow and falling as in the end of October. In short, Twickenham is rueful; I don't believe Westphalia looks more barren. Nay, we are forced to fortify ourselves too. Hanworth was broken open last night, though the family was all there. Lord Vere lost a silver standish, an old watch, and his writing-box with fifty pounds in it. They broke it open in the park, but missed a diamond ring, which was found, and the telescope, which by the weight of the case they had fancied full of money. Another house in the middle of Sunbury has had the same fate. I am mounting cannon on my battlements.

Your château I hope, proceeds faster than mine. The carpenters are all associated for increase of wages; I have had but two men at work these five weeks. You know, to be sure, that Lady Mary Wortley cannot live. Adieu, my dear Lord!"

"To Henry Seymour Conway,   Strawberry Hill, 9 September 1762
..... all my glories were on the point of vanishing last night in a flame! The chimney of the new Gallery, which chimney is full of deal-boards, and which Gallery is full of shavings, was on fire at eight o'clock. Harry had quarrelled with the other servants, and would not sit in the kitchen; and to keep up his anger had lighted a vast fire in the servants' hall, which is under the gallery. The chimney took fire; and if Margaret had not smelt it with the first nose that ever a servant had, a quarter of an hour had set us in a blaze. I hope you are frightened out of your senses for me ....."

"To George Montagu,   Strawberry Hill, 1 July 1763
..... I quit the gallery almost in the critical minute of consummation. Gilders, carvers, upholsterers, and picture-cleaners are labouring at their several forges, and I do not love to trust a hammer or a brush without my own supervisal ....."

"To George Montagu,   Strawberry Hill, 15 August 1763
The most important piece of news that I have to tell you, is, that the gallery is finished; that is, the workmen have quitted it. For chairs and tables, not one is arrived yet. Well! how you will tramp up and down in it! – methinks, I wish you would. We are in the perfection of beauty; verdure itself was

never green till this summer, thanks to the deluges of rain. Our complexion used to be mahogany in August. Nightingales and roses indeed are out of blow, but the season is celestial. I don't know whether we have not even had an earthquake today. Lady Buckingham, Lady Waldegrave, the Bishop of Exeter and Mrs Keppel, and the little Hotham dined here; between six and seven we were sitting in the great parlour, I sat in the window looking at the river. On a sudden I saw it violently agitated, and as it were lifted up and down by a thousand hands. I called out, they all ran to the window; it continued; we hurried into the garden, all saw the Thames in the same violent commotion for I suppose an hundred yards ....."

"To The Earl of Hertford,   Strawberry Hill, 3 August 1764
..... I have been much distressed this morning. The royal family reside chiefly at Richmond, whither scarce necessary servants attend them, and no mortal else but Lord Bute. The King and Queen have taken to going about to see places; they have been at Oatlands and Wanstead. A quarter before ten to-day, I heard the bell at the gate ring, – truth is, I was not up, for my hours are not reformed, either at night or in the morning, – I inquired who it was? the Prince of Mecklenburgh and De Witz had called to know if they could see the house; my two Swiss, Favre and Louis, told them I was in bed, but if they would call again in an hour, they might see it. I shuddered at this report, – and would it were the worst part! The Queen herself was behind, in a coach: I am shocked to death, and know not what to do! It is ten times worse just now than ever at any other time: it will certainly be said, that I refused to let the Queen see my house. See what it is to have republican servants! When I made a tempest about it, Favre said, with the utmost sang froid, 'why could not he tell me he was the Prince of Mecklenburgh?' I shall go this evening and consult my oracle, Lady Suffolk. If she approves it, I will write to De Witz, and pretend I know nothing of anybody but the Prince, and beg a thousand pardons, and assure him how proud I should be to have his master visit my castle at Thundertentronk."

*H*e describes below the writing of his best known work *The Castle of Otranto*. It was a great success and has run to over one hundred and fifty editions since it was first published anonymously in 1764. It is regarded as the first Gothic novel, an enjoyable horror story, inspiring a cult that gave rise to works by Mary Shelley and others; even Jane Austen's 'Northanger Abbey' owes its existence to Otranto. As well as using Strawberry Hill as the castle in which the plot is set, Walpole used one of the Cambridge colleges, probably Trinity, to provide background material for the Great Hall of Otranto, the Chapel and Gate.

It is this work (together with his *Anecdotes of Painting*) with which Walpole was most satisfied. In it he was able not only to recreate Strawberry's Gothic features but also to introduce heraldry and all the elements of the Middle Ages that he found most satisfying; for the six weeks of writing it he entered a period in which he would have liked to live. When it was finished he chose to have it printed as a Renaissance manuscript translated by "William Marshal, Gent. from the original Italian of Onuphrio Muralto, Canon of the Church of St. Nicholas at Otranto", and stated that it had been written in 1529. By April 1765, after the success of the first edition, no longer afraid of being ridiculed, he republished with a dedication signed H.W. These initials were enough to inform the public of the identity of the author; however, the nom de plume Onuphrio Muralto might have given a clue to his authorship – intentionally or otherwise – it is loosely in the form of an anagram and may have revealed his identity to his friends. This first anonymous edition was much later to result in controversy regarding the poet, Chatterton, and to cause Walpole much unease and unhappiness.

His intention in writing *Otranto* was to write a tale of chivalry which was made palatable to the 18th century reader by creating characters who spoke in everyday language however extraordinary the situations in which they were placed, and also through telling what might later be called 'a ripping good yarn'. It took an immediate hold on society in much the same way as Conan Doyle's Sherlock Holmes stories did in the 19th century. In his second preface to the book Walpole described it as "an attempt to blend the two kinds of romance: the ancient and the modern."

"To the Rev. William Cole,   Strawberry Hill, 9 March 1765
Dear Sir,
I had time to write but a short note with the *Castle of Otranto*, as your messenger called on me at four o'clock, as I was going to dine abroad. Your partiality to me and Strawberry have, I hope, inclined you to excuse the wildness of the story. You will even have found some traits to put you in mind of this place. When you read of the picture quitting its panel, did not you recollect the portrait of Lord Falkland, all in white, in my gallery? Shall

I even confess to you, what was the origin of this romance! I waked one morning, in the beginning of last June, from a dream, of which, all I could recover was, that I had thought myself in an ancient castle (a very natural dream for a head filled like mine with Gothic story), and that on the upper-most bannister of a great staircase I saw a gigantic hand in armour. In the evening I sat down, and began to write, without knowing in the least what I intended to say or relate. The work grew on my hands, and I grew fond of it – add, that I was very glad to think of anything, rather than politics. in short, I was so engrossed with my tale, which I completed in less than two months, that one evening, I wrote from the time I had drunk my tea, about six o'clock, till half an hour after one in the morning, when my hands and fingers were so weary, that I could not hold the pen to finish the sentence, but left Matilda and Isabella talking, in the middle of a paragraph. You will laugh at my earnestness; but if I have amused you, by retracing with any fidelty the manners of ancient days, I am content, and give you leave to think me as idle as you please ....."

"To George Montagu,   Strawberry Hill, 10 June 1765
                                                eleven at night
I am just come out of the garden in the most oriental of all evenings, and from breathing odours beyond those of Araby. The acacias, which the Arabians have the sense to worship, are covered with blossoms, the honeysuckles

dangle from every tree in festoons, the seringas are thickets of sweets, and the new–cut hay in the field tempers the balmy gales with simple freshness; while a thousand sky-rockets launched into the air at Ranelagh or Marybone illuminate the scene, and give it an air of Haroun Alraschid's paradise. I was not quite so content by daylight; some foreigners dined here, and, though they admired our verdure, it mortified me by its brownness – we have not had a drop of rain this month to cool the tip of our daisies ....."

"To the Right Hon. Lady Hervey,   Strawberry Hill, 11 June 1765
I am almost as much ashamed, Madam, to plead the true cause of my faults towards your ladyship, as to have been guilty of any neglect. It is scandalous, at my age, to have been carried backwards and forwards to balls and suppers and parties by very young people, as I was all last week. My resolutions of growing old and staid are admirable: I wake with a sober plan, and intend to pass the day with my friends – then comes the Duke of Richmond, and hurries me down to Whitehall to dinner – then the Duchess of Grafton sends for me to loo in Upper Grosvenor street – before I can get thither, I am begged to step to Kensington, to give Mrs. Anne Pitt my opinion about a bow-window – after the loo, I am to march back to Whitehall to supper – and after that, I am to walk with Miss Pelham on the terrace till two in the morning, because it is moonlight and her chair is not come. All this does not help my morning laziness; and, by the time I have breakfasted, fed my birds and my squirrels, and dressed, there is an auction ready. In short, Madam, this was my life last week, and is I think every week, with the addition of forty episodes. – Yet, ridiculous as it is, I send it your ladyship, because I had rather you should laugh at me than be angry. I cannot offend you in intention, but I fear my sins of omission are equal to many a good Christian's. Pray forgive me. I really will begin to be between forty and fifty by the time I am fourscore: and I truly believe I will bring my resolutions within compass; for I have not chalked out any particular business that will take me above forty years more; so that, if I do not get acquainted with the grandchildren of all the present age, I shall lead a quiet sober life yet before I die ....."

From the time of the Grand Tour Walpole was a francophile and in the two letters below he gives some reasons for his frequent visits to Paris. He bought much of the china that was displayed or used at Strawberry Hill in Paris and in November 1765, having gone to France on an extended visit with his friend, William Cole, he together with Cole and the Duke and Duchess of Richmond visited the Sèvres porcelain factory where he purchased a number of pieces. On the 1765 trip, Walpole made two visits to Sèvres buying eight objects and spending 378 livres, however it was more normal for him to buy French porcelain from one of the fashionable marchands-merciers of Paris – where he could choose from the output of different factories and compare styles and designs of porcelain, enamels and other luxury objects d'art.

"To George Montagu,   Strawberry Hill, 31 August 1765

..... I go to see French plays and buy French china, not to know their ministers, to look into their government, or think of the interests of nations – in short, unlike most people that are growing old, I am convinced that nothing is charming but what appeared important in one's youth, which afterwards passes for follies ....."

"To The Right Hon. Lady Hervey,   Paris, 15 September 1765

I am but two days old here, Madam, and I doubt I wish I was really so, and had my life to begin, to live it here. You see how just I am, and ready to make amende honorable to your Ladyship. Yet I have seen very little. My Lady Hertford has cut me to pieces, and thrown me into a caldron with tailors, periwig-makers, snuff-box-wrights, milliners, etc., which really took up but little time; and I am come out quite new, with everything but youth. The journey recovered me with magic expedition. My strength, if mine could ever be called strength, is returned; and the gout going off in a minuet step. I will say nothing of my spirits, which are indecently juvenile, and not less improper for my age than for the country where I am; which, if you will give me leave to say it, has a thought too much gravity. I don't venture to laugh or talk nonsense, but in English.

Madame Geoffrin came to town but last night, and is not visible on Sundays; but I hope to deliver your ladyship's letter and packet to-morrow. Mesdames d'Aiguillon, d'Egmont, and Chabot, and the Duc de Nivernois are all in the country. Madame de Boufflers is at l'Isle Adam, whither my Lady Hertford is gone to–night to sup, for the first time, being no longer chained down to the incivility of an ambassadress. She returns after supper; an irregularity that frightens me, who have not yet got rid of all my barbarisms. There is one, alas! I never shall get over the dirt of this country: it is melancholy, after the purity of Strawberry! The narrowness of the streets, trees clipped to resemble brooms, and planted on pedestals of chalk, and a few other points, do not edify me. The French Opera, which I have heard to-night, disgusted me as much as ever; and the more for being followed by the 'Devin de Village', which shows that they can sing without cracking the drum of one's ear. the scenes and dances are delightful: the Italian comedy charming. Then I am in love with treillage and fountains, and will prove it at Strawberry. Chantilly is so exactly what it was when I saw it above twenty years ago, that I recollected the very position of Monsieur le Duc's chair and the gallery. The latter gave me the first idea for mine; but, presumption apart, mine is a thousand times prettier ....."

"To George Montagu,   Paris, 5 January 1766
..... It is pleasing to have life painted with images by the pencil of friendship. Visions, you know, have always been my pasture; and so far from growing old enough to quarrel with their emptiness, I almost think there is no wisdom comparable to that of exchanging what is called the realities of life for dreams. Old castles, old pictures, old histories, and the babble of old people make one live back into centuries that cannot disappoint one. One holds fast and surely what is past .....

                                                        9 January
I had not sent away my letter, being disappointed of a messenger, and now receive yours of December 30th. My house is most heartily at your service, and I shall write to Favre to have it ready for you. You will see by the former part of this letter, that I do not think of being in England before the end of March. All I dislike in this contract, is, the fear, that if I drive you out of my house, I shall drive you out of town; and as you will find, I have not a bed to offer you but my own, and Favre's, in which your servant will lie, for I have stripped Arlington Street to furnish Strawberry. In the meantime, you will be comfortable in my bed, and need have no trouble about Favre, as he lodges at his wife's, while I am absent. Let them know in time to have the beds aired ....."

On his return to England Walpole continued building and decorating the Round Tower which he had first started in 1760. The Gothic sources that he suggested Robert Adam should use were engraved by Wenceslaus Hollar and illustrated in Dugdale's 'History of St Paul's Cathedral in London' published in 1658, and Dart's 'Westmonasterium'. The room was never used as a bedchamber.

"To Robert Adam,   26 September 1766
Mr. Walpole has sent Mr. Adam the two books, and hopes at his leisure he will think of the ceiling and chimney-piece. The ceiling is to be taken from the plate 165 of St. Paul's, the circular window.

The chimney from the shrine of Edward the Confessor, at Westminster. The diameter of the room is 22 feet. The enclosed little end is for the bed, which Mr. Walpole begs to have drawn out too. He is just going to Bath, and will call on Mr. Adam as soon as he returns."

In the next letter, written to William Cole, Walpole mentions that he had to have "bespoke" windows. With one exception the windows of Strawberry Hill all have shutters which slide back into the wall space when not in use, and their design must have been included in the original building specifications. The shutters became more complex as the building programme progressed; thus the Blue Breakfast Room, adapted with ogee windows by Walpole from the Chopp'd Straw Hall room, has no ogee on the shutters and they are simply made. The next rooms to be completed, Library and Great Parlour, had shutters made reflecting the room designs; refinements were added in the Great Parlour to eliminate draughts and securely lock this room which is on the ground floor. The Round Room when completed by Adam had very sophisticated shutters shaped to complete the circle of the Tower and to form part of the decor of the room; they form a moveable screen and must frequently have been kept in position across the windows to enhance the atmosphere of the room and to prevent light fading the delicate fabrics covering the furniture and walls.

✢ ✢ ✢

Walpole was always fascinated by Royalty, but he was partial. He approved of the Plantagenets, collected the portraits of them that had hung in Shene Palace and elsewhere and rehung them in his Armoury at Strawberry Hill, where they increased the medieval atmosphere. They represented for him the greatest period of chivalry. He sought to clear Richard III, Yorkist and Plantagenet, from the Shakespearean slur of the mass murder of everyone standing between Richard and the throne. His *Historic Doubts on the Life and Reign of King Richard III* published in 1768 was a spirited defence of the King, but his research and immediate reasons for writing the book were unfortunately based on shaky scholarship. He had found a 15th century document, which he believed to be the Coronation Roll of Richard III, with mention of the sons of Edward IV at a time when they were thought to be dead, presumably murdered by Richard III, their 'wicked uncle', thereby, Walpole believed, confirming their existence in 1484. He was mistaken; the Roll proved only to be a wardrobe account to which no dates could be firmly attached and therefore could not stand up to the interpretation given it by Walpole.

Morton, Bishop of Ely, author of the majority of source material on Richard, is described by Walpole as follows: "Morton had not only violated his allegiance to Richard; but had been the chief engine to dethrone him, and to plant a bastard scyon in the throne. Of all men living there could not be more suspicious testimony than the prelate's except the King's", (Henry VII). The book followed publication of his Gothic novel *The Castle of Otranto* and is very much another Gothic tale, with historical fact cloaked in mystery. Walpole's enjoyment of the horror can be felt throughout the text. It provoked discussion, argument and became an instant success when published; 1,200 copies sold immediately and Dodsley, the publisher, started a second run of 1,000 copies. The more Walpole was attacked by disbelieving readers the more stubbornly he stood by his new interpretation of the events. This is the debate about which today historians still argue; was Richard the hunchback Shakespearean monster or was he innocent of crime, perhaps a great king? Were the princes, his nephews, murdered by Richard, Henry, Buckingham or someone else altogether? Walpole was a man of extremes, for him it was black or white; there could not be a middle path. Here Walpole is delighted to receive an opportunity to attack his critics through Cole.

"To the Rev. William Cole,   Strawberry Hill, 6 June 1768
You have told me what makes me both sorry and glad: long have I expected the appearance of Ely, and thought it on the eve of coming forth! Now you tell me it is not half written – but then I am rejoiced that you are to write it. Pray do; the author is very much in the right to make you author for him. I cannot say you have addressed yourself quite so judiciously as he has. I never heard of Cardinal Lewis of Luxembourg in my days, nor have a scrap of the history of Normandy, but Ducarel's tour to the Conqueror's kitchen. But your best way will be to come and rummage my library yourself; not to set me to writing the lives of prelates; I shall strip them stark, and you will have them to re-consecrate. Cardinal Morton is at your service: pray, say for him and of me, what you please. I have very slender opinion of his integrity, but as I am not spiteful, it would be hard to exact from you a less favourable account of him, than I conclude your piety will bestow on all his predecessors and successors. Seriously you know how little I take contradiction to heart, and beg you will have no scruples about defending Morton. When I bestow but a momentary smile on the abuse of my answerers, I am not likely to stint a friend in a fair and obliging remark. The man whom you mention that calls himself 'Impartialis', is I suppose some hackney historian, I shall never inquire whom, angry at being censored in the lump, and not named. I foretold he would drop his criticisms before he entered on Perkin Warbeck, which I knew he could not answer, and so it happened – good night to him!
      Unfortunately I am no culinary antiquary: the Bishop of Carlisle, who is, I have oft heard talk of a 'sotelte', as an ancient dish. He is rambling between London, Hagley, and Carlisle, that I do not know where to consult

him; but if the book is not printed before winter, I am sure he could translate your bill of fare into modern phrase. As I trust I shall see you here some time this summer, you might bring your papers with you, and we will try what we can make of them. Tell me, do, when it will be most convenient to you to come from now to the end of October. At the same time I will beg to see the letters of the University to King Richard: and shall be still more obliged to you for the print of Jane Shore. I have a very bad mezzotinto of her, either from the picture at Cambridge or Eton.

I wish I could return these favours by contributing to the decoration of your 'new old' house; but as you know, I erected an old house, not demolished one, I had no windows or frames for windows but what I bespoke on purpose for the places where they are. My painted glass was so exhausted, before I had got through my design, that I was forced to have the windows in the gallery painted on purpose by Pecket. What scraps I have remaining are so bad, I cannot make you pay for the carriage of them, as I think there is not one whole piece, but you shall see them when you come hither, and I will search if I can find anything for your purpose – I am sure I owe it to you. Adieu!"

"To Sir William Hamilton,   Strawberry Hill, 22 September 1768
Dear Sir,

I have just been a progress with Mr. Conway to Lord Hertford's, Lord Strafford's and other places, and at my return three days ago found the cases arrived. I tore them open with the utmost impatience, and cannot describe how agreeably I was surprised to find the contents so much beyond my expectation. They are not only beautiful in themselves and well preserved, but the individual things I should have wished for, if I had known they existed. For this year past I have been projecting a chimney in imitation of the tomb of Edward the Confessor, and had partly given it up, on finding how enormously expensive it would be. Mr. Adam had drawn me a design a little in that style, prettier it is true, and at half the price. I had actually agreed to have it executed in scagliola, but have just heard that the man complained he could not perform his compact for the money settled. Your obliging present is I am certain executed by the very person who made the Confessor's monument; and if the scagliola-

man wishes to be off his bargain, I shall be glad; if not, still these materials
will make me a beautiful chimney-piece for another room. I again give you
ten thousand thanks for them, dear Sir. I value them for themselves, and
much more for the person they came from ....."

The following letter is written to Chatterton, it forms one in a sequence which
describes one of the most unhappy episodes in Walpole's life. Chatterton was
born in Bristol in 1752. He became, like Walpole, engrossed in the Middle Ages
and wrote to Walpole, as the writer and publisher of *Anecdotes of Painting in
England,* with extracts of works which expounded the theory that the art of oil
painting had been discovered by a medieval monk named Rowley, at a time
which predated the oil paintings of the Van Eycks, who are normally credited
with developing the technique. Walpole considered the first letter to be genuine,
but shortly after receiving it showed the supposedly 'medieval' poems to
Thomas Gray and other friends who pointed out anachronisms. Walpole then
ceased all correspondence with Chatterton; the boy came to London and took
his own life shortly afterwards in 1770 by taking arsenic. Many people at the
time considered Walpole morally responsible for his death, and because he had
waited two years before answering accusations, at first believing it unnecessary
to do so, his statement of fact and plea of innocence when it finally came, were
too late to be accepted. Chatterton's fabrication of Rowley the monk was
compared to Walpole's publication of *The Castle of Otranto* supposedly written
by Onuphrio Muralto. The incident itself and the death of the boy poet
remained on his mind and he returned to the subject many times justifying
himself and restating the facts.

"To Mr. Thomas Chatterton,   Arlington Street, 28 March 1769
Sir,

I cannot but think myself singularly obliged by a gentleman with whom I
have not the pleasure of being acquainted, when I read your very curious
and kind letter, which I have this minute received. I give you a thousand
thanks for it, and for the very obliging offer you make me, of communicat-
ing your MSS. to me. What you have already sent me is very valuable, and
full of information; but instead of correcting you, Sir, you are far more able
to correct me. I have not the happiness of understanding the Saxon
language, and without your learned notes should not have been able to
comprehend Rowley's text.

As a second edition of my *Anecdotes* was published but last year, I must
not flatter myself that a third will be wanted soon; but I shall be happy to
lay up any notices you will be so good as to extract from me, and send me
at your leisure; for, as it is uncertain when I may use them, I would by no

means borrow and detain your MSS.

Give me leave to ask you where Rowley's poems are to be found? I should not be sorry to print them; or at least, a specimen of them, if they have never been printed.

The Abbot John's verses that you have given me, are wonderful for their harmony and spirit, though there are some words I do not understand.

You do not point out exactly the time when he lived, which I wish to know, as I suppose it was long before John Ab Eyck's discovery of oil-painting. If so, it confirms what I had guessed, and have hinted in my *Anecdotes*, that oil-painting was known here much earlier than that discovery or revival.

I will not trouble you with more questions now, Sir, but flatter myself from the humanity and politeness you have already shown me, that you will sometimes give me leave to consult you. I hope, too, you will forgive the simplicity of my direction, as you have favoured me with no other.

I am, Sir,

Your much obliged

And obedient humble servant,

Hor. Walpole."

"To George Montagu, Arlington Street, 11 May 1769

..... Strawberry has been in great glory; I have given a festino there that will almost mortgage it. Last Tuesday all France dined there: monsieur and Madame du Châtelet, the Duc de Liancour, three more French ladies, whose names you will find in the enclosed paper, eight other Frenchmen, the Spanish and Portuguese ministers, the Holdernesses, Fitzroys, in short we were four and twenty. They arrived at two. At the gates of the castle I received them, dressed in the cravat of Gibbons's carving, and a pair of gloves embroidered up to the elbows that had belonged to James I. The French servants stared, and firmly believed this was the dress of English country gentlemen. After taking a survey of the apartments, we went to the printing-house, where I had prepared the enclosed verses, with translations by Monsieur de Lille, one of the company. The moment they were printed off, I gave a private signal, and French horns and clarionets accompanied this compliment. We then went to see Pope's grotto and garden, and returned to a magnificent dinner in the refectory. In the evening we walked, had tea, coffee, and lemonade in the Gallery, which was illuminated with a thousand, or thirty candles, I forget which, and played at whisk and loo till midnight. Then there was a cold supper, and at one the company returned to town, saluted by fifty nightingales, who, as tenants of the manor, came to do honour to their lord ....."

Whenever possible Walpole avoided paying heavy import duty on the china he purchased in France by getting it transported via the diplomatic bag.

"To George Montagu,   Strawberry Hill, 16 October, 1769
I arrived at my own Louvre last Wednesday night, and am now at my Versailles. Your last letter reached me but two days before I left Paris, for I have been an age at Calais and upon the sea. I could execute no commission for you, and, in truth, you gave me no explicit one; but I have brought you a bit of china, and beg you will be content with a little present, instead of a bargain. Said china is, or will be soon, in the Custom House; but I shall have it, I fear, long before you come to London .....

I feel myself here like a swan, that, after living six weeks in a nasty pool upon a common, is got back into its own Thames. I do nothing but plume and clean myself, and enjoy the verdure and silent waves. Neatness and greenth are so essential in my opinion to the country, that in France, where I see nothing but chalk and dirty peasants, I seem in a terrestrial purgatory that is neither town nor country. The face of England is so beautiful, that I do not believe Tempe or Arcadia were half so rural; for both lying in hot climates, must have wanted the turf of our lawns. It is unfortunate to have so pastoral a taste, when I want a cane more than a crook. We are absurd creatures; at twenty, I loved nothing but London.

Tell me when you shall be in town. I think of passing most of my time here till after Christmas. Adieu!"

Strawberry had become his main home even in winter, and spaniels were a feature of life there; Walpole was fond of them and mentions them frequently in his letters. He took a favourite, Tory, on the Grand Tour with him where the dog was seized by a wolf when the party was crossing the Alps. There is a watercolour of Walpole sitting in the Library reading with a dog beside his chair, another spaniel curls up asleep in the painted glass of the Little Parlour, two more can be found in the glass of the Tribune, more are in the Blue Room glass and one explanation for the mysteriously low height of the dado rail in the Great Parlour is that it may have been placed at spaniel height to keep the walls clean – Cavalier King Charles spaniels tend to dry themselves, when wet, by rubbing against walls, and Walpole's dogs must have spent a lot of time in the Thames at the bottom of the garden.

"To Sir Horace Mann,   Arlington Street, 23 March 1770
You know I have always some favourite, some successor of Patapan. The present is a tanned black spaniel, called Rosette. She

saved my life last Saturday night, so I am sure you will love her too. I was undressing for bed. She barked and was so restless that there was no quieting her. I fancied there was somebody under the bed, but there was not. As she looked at the chimney, which roared much, I thought it was the wind, yet wondered, as she had heard it so often. At last, not being able to quiet her, I looked to see what she barked at, and perceived sparks of fire falling from the chimney, and on searching farther perceived it in flames. It had not gone far, and we easily extinguished it. I wish I had as much power over the nation's chimney. Adieu!"

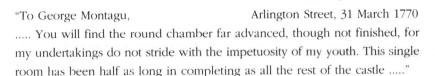

"To George Montagu,   Arlington Street, 31 March 1770

..... You will find the round chamber far advanced, though not finished, for my undertakings do not stride with the impetuosity of my youth. This single room has been half as long in completing as all the rest of the castle ....."

In the following letter Walpole lists some of the most fashionable goods and pastimes available in the 18th century and gives an amusing account of the new practice of holding 'exhibitions' where objects were displayed for sale. He had his own collection of English portraits in print form – 12,000 of them – which he showed to his visitors. By 1770 Strawberry Hill had become a small house bursting at the seams with the enormous number of items housed within it.

"To Sir Horace Mann,   Strawberry Hill, 6 May 1770

..... There has lately been an auction of stuffed birds; and, as natural history is in fashion, there are physicians and others who paid forty and fifty guineas for a single Chinese pheasant: you may buy a live one for five. After this, it is not extraordinary that pictures should be dear. We have at present three exhibitions. One West, who paints history in the taste of Poussin, gets three hundred pounds for a piece not too large to hang over a chimney. He has merit, but is hard and heavy, and far unworthy of such prices. The rage to see these exhibitions is so great, that sometimes one cannot pass through the streets where they are. But it is incredible what sums are raised by mere exhibitions of anything; a new fashion, and to enter at which you pay a shilling or half-a-crown. Another rage, is for prints of English portraits: I have been collecting them above thirty years, and originally never gave for a

mezzotinto above one or two shillings. The lowest are now a crown; most, from half a guinea to a guinea. Lately, I assisted a clergyman in compiling a catalogue of them; since the publication, scarce heads in books, not worth threepence, will sell for five guineas. Then we have Etruscan vases, made of earthenware, in Staffordshire, from two to five guineas; and or moulu never made here before, which succeeds so well, that a tea-kettle, which the inventor offered for 100 guineas, sold by auction for 130. In short, we are at the height of extravagance and improvements, for we do improve rapidly in taste as well as in the former. I cannot say so much for our genius. Poetry is gone to bed, or into our prose; we are like the Romans in that too. If we have the arts of the Antonines, – we have the fustian also ..... Adieu!"

In 1774 Walpole first published *A Description of the Villa of Mr Horace Walpole at Strawberry Hill near Twickenham, Middlesex with an inventory of the Furniture, Pictures, Curiosities Etc.* It is a catalogue and account of his purchases listing, where appropriate, from which earlier collections they had come. He compares this act of provenance to that of the genealogy of the race horse, but considered it not as noble as the blood line of the peerage. He describes also the mixing of antique with modern and suggests it may seem "heterogeneous. In truth", he goes on, "I did not mean to make my house so Gothic as to exclude convenience and modern refinement in luxury. The designs of the inside and outside are strictly ancient, but the decorations are modern."

The Preface to the *Description* opens with the paragraph: "It will look, I fear, a little like arrogance in a private man to give a printed description of his villa and collection, in which almost every thing is diminutive. It is not, however, intended for public sale, and originally was meant only to assist those who would visit the place. A farther view succeeded; that of exhibiting specimens of Gothic architecture, as collected from standards in cathedrals and chapel-tombs, and showing how they may be applied to chimney-pieces, ceilings, windows, balustrades, loggias, etc. The general disuse of Gothic architecture, and the decay and alterations so frequently made in churches, give prints a chance of being the sole preservatives of that style". The reader is taken, room by room, through the house with every item listed. As the work was updated and amended it probably provides the single most valuable source for any study of Walpole or the 18th century collectors' interior.

✦✦✦

China was one of the areas which most interested Walpole and the Collection at Strawberry Hill was representative of the developments in the industry through the second half of the 18th century, but it neither accurately reflected aristocratic taste nor did it display the themes that were found in the rest of the Collection.

The *Description* of the house is the best source for investigating what he owned, but his terminology in keeping with the time was lax, and it is easy to make assumptions which may be quite inaccurate. For example, he rarely distinguishes between Chinese and Japanese ware, or 'old' blue and white and their English copies. So an Imari piece was called Japan ware by Walpole, even if it came from China. A piece of "old Delft ware" seems to describe any piece of pottery and "Etruscan vases made in Staffordshire" almost certainly stood for Wedgwood pieces. In the 1784 *Description* he lists a piece kept in the china closet of the house as a "Tuscan vase of Wedgwood's ware". However, Roman copies of Etruscan ware were also to be found in the Collection again described as Etruscan, so the difficulty of sorting ancient from modern is apparent.

He owned many early Wedgwood pieces including several decorated with designs by Lady Diana Beauclerc, among them "12 plates of Wedgwood's ware, with cameos of blue and white and blue festoons; a design by Lady Diana Beauclerc". The matching "12 plates" are unusual because he normally chose not to have sets of dishes or plates, but in the spirit of the true collector fascinated by the rapid development in china, picked the best items from the factories of Europe for use as well as for display, rather than follow the contemporary trend of acquiring sets or services. To buy French ceramics he visited the factory at Sèvres and listed the items he chose very carefully. 18th century Sèvres ware was fashionable, particularly the pink and green wares mounted in ormolu, but Walpole preferred the dark blue and also bought several pieces in purple, now considered very rare. In the Holbein Chamber he lists, "two bottles of Roman fayence, and a bason and ewer of purple and white Seve china." In the Great North Bedchamber stood Sèvres Incense Burners, shaped like snails – rare items both for Walpole and Sèvres; although he loved animals, and was always discussing them in his letters he only very occasionally bought a decorative piece of an animal, when he did it seems to have been because it represented something other than the animal itself. This was the period when figures were fashionable but he probably bought the snails because they were a rarity when in the form of incense burners, an item which itself was becoming increasingly popular towards the end of the century with continuing interest in all items oriental. He also bought from Sèvres a large garniture in turquoise blue with festoons of ormolu ornament, costing nineteen guineas; this was the colour favoured by Catherine the Great when she bought from Sèvres in 1779. He tried and failed to buy from them a cup in imitation of lapis lazuli.

He bought china from Meissen, calling it "Saxon Ware", but he bought no typical figures from them, for which they were famous. The nearest he came to one was a Böttger piece of "a boy supporting a shell, finely modelled in red earth; the first sort of saxon china before it was glazed or painted, and which was given as presents by the Elector; extremely rare". This piece appears to have been kept by him, together with other odd or experimental pieces, because it marked a transitional stage of development in the making of porcelain. In other words he appeared to want his ceramics collection to reflect the growth and development of the industry and the changing techniques. This is not the way in which he viewed other items in his collection.

From the Chelsea factory he bought twelve plates decorated with coloured birds and twelve more painted with fruit and flowers – all different – which he used for entertaining together with Chelsea salt cellars; this was fairly unusual because generally silver salts were still being used. Also from the Chelsea factory came the set of "handle" cups and saucers, decorated with green landscapes on a white ground, of which he was immensely proud – tea cups with handles were still new. Again, he had no fashionable figures from Chelsea, but published his attitude to figures, their uses, and the over-decoration of china in 1753 when he wrote in 'The World' on the subject of embellishment of dessert dishes; "Jellies, biscuits, sugar-plums, and creams have long given way to harlequins, gondoliers, Turks, Chinese, and Shepherdesses of Saxon china..... by degrees, whole meadows of cattle, of the same brittle materials, spread themselves over the whole table; cottages rose in sugar, and temples in barley sugar; the pigmy Neptunes in cars of cockle-shells triumphed over oceans of looking-glass or seas of Silver Tissue". He owned many European pieces painted with birds; Duvivier, a painter who worked for a time at Sèvres and specialised in painting exotic birds, came to England and worked for a period at the Chelsea, New Hall and Worcester factories. Walpole had several pieces which, from their descriptions, could have been painted by him. It is possible to speculate that he may have admired Duvivier's work and bought from the factories which sold his painted bird wares.

From Josiah Wedgwood, in addition to items of "Tuscan" ware and those decorated after designs by Lady Diana Beauclerc, he bought the new hard wearing creamware, which had a glossy and long lasting cream glaze, later called Queen's Ware, and plates painted and decorated in the form of leaves. Wedgwood, and his partner Thomas Bentley, took showrooms at the corner of St Martin's Lane where also could be found the furniture workshops and show-room where some of the furniture designed by Richard Bentley of Walpole's Committee of Taste (but no relation), was made up. The china clay and stone first used by Josiah Wedgwood, and developed into Queen's Ware, was found on land belonging to Thomas Pitt from whom eventually they received a lease for digging china clay. Pitt was Chatham's nephew, a friend of Walpole, and involved in the design of the Gallery at Strawberry Hill. There appears therefore to be several connections between Wedgwood and the Strawberry Hill set.

Horace Walpole seems to have been fascinated by the decoration and detail of ceramics as well as its technical development, even if he didn't always approve, "an old blue and white plate with a rib in the middle", or a teapot of quilted china of St. Cloud, or a triangular salt cellar of "Fayence", all items that would be the centre of conversation. The China Collection was representative of all the main factories in Europe, and in it he traced the development of true porcelain from soft paste. This is unexpected.

The best pieces of the Collection were not kept in the China Closet on the ground floor of the house which held everyday china, but in the Round Room, in the small china closet off the Round Room, and in the wig cupboard of the Great North Bedchamber, all of which are on the first or principal floor; illustrations of some of the pieces can be seen in John Carter's watercolours of the interior of the house.

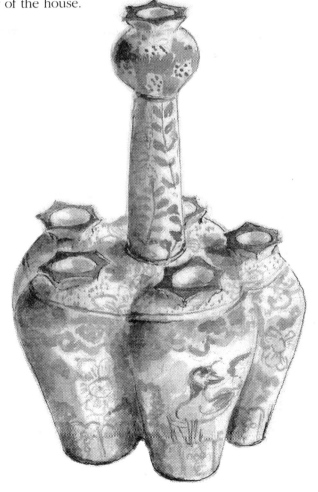

*W*alpole was a small eater, drank iced water and only rarely took wine, yet he suffered badly from gout which was considered a fashionable ailment in the 18th century. Some attacks were so severe that he had to be carried around his house by his staff.

"To George Montagu,   Strawberry Hill, 3 October 1770
I am going on in the sixth week of my fit, and having had a return this morning in my knee, I cannot flatter myself with any approaching prospect of recovery. The gate of painful age seems open to me, and I must travel through it as I may!

If you have not written one word for another, I am at a loss to understand you. You say you have taken a house in London for a year, that you are gone to Waldeshare for six months, and then you shall come for the winter. Either you mean six weeks, or differ from most people in reckoning April the beginning of winter. I hope your pen was in a hurry, rather than your calculation so uncommon. I certainly shall be glad of your residing in London. I have long wished to live nearer to you, but it was in happier days – I am now so dismayed by these returns of gout, that I can promise myself few comforts in any future scenes of my life. I am much obliged to Lord Guilford and Lord North, and was very sorry that the latter came to see Strawberry in so bad a day, and when I was so extremely ill and full of pain, that I scarce knew he was here; and as my coachman was gone to London to fetch me bootikins, there was no carriage to offer him – but indeed in the condition I then was, I was not capable of doing any of the honours of my house, suffering at once in my hand, knee, and both feet. I am still lifted out of bed by two servants, and by their help travel from my bedchamber down to the couch in my blue room – but I shall conclude, rather than tire you with so unpleasant a history. Adieu!

Yours ever

H.W."

The state bedchamber in the next letter became known as the Great North Bedchamber when finished. Next to the chimney a trompe l'oeil window can be seen today dating from the period before the building of the bedchamber, when the fireplace wall was the exterior wall of the Long Gallery facing the main road. It was impossible for Walpole to have built windows on the road side of the Gallery because the wall was solid, panelled in mirrors.

This, like the Hall trompe l'oeil, reflects the practice in Genoa of dealing with windows on a Long Gallery mirrored wall.

"To Sir Horace Mann,   Strawberry Hill, 8 June 1771

..... How happy it would make me to see you here, salva your dignitate. Strawberry is in the most perfect beauty, the verdure exquisite, and the shades venerably extended. I have made a Gothic gateway to the garden, the piers of which are of artificial stone and very respectable. The round tower is finished and magnificent; and the state bedchamber proceeds fast – for you must know the little villa is grown into a superb castle .....

My party ..... succeeded to admiration, and Gothic architecture has received great applause – I will not swear that it has been really admired – I found by Monsieur de Guisnes that though he had heard much of the house, it was in no favourable light. He had been told it was only built of lathe and plaster, and that there were not two rooms together on a level. When I once asked Madame du Deffand what her countrymen said of it, she owned they were not struck with it, but looked upon it as natural enough in a country, which had not yet arrived at true taste. In short, I believe they think all the houses they see are Gothic, because they are not like that single pattern that reigns in every hôtel in Paris, and which made me say there, that I never knew whether I was in the house I was in, or the house I came out of ....."

In 1771 Walpole returned to Paris to buy more for his Collection. He writes "Heaps of glorious works by Raphael and all the great masters are piled up and equally neglected" by the French nobility.

The armour described in the next letter was bought by him and stood within a niche in the Armoury of Strawberry Hill, where it became one of his most treasured possessions. Walpole believed it had been made by Benvenuto Cellini, the Renaissance gold and silversmith, for Francis I of France, and he even bought the armour of Francis' horse to complete the image; however it is now thought that it neither belonged to the French King, nor was it made by Cellini. The niche in the Armoury in which it was displayed was discovered only recently during restoration work in the house.

❖ ❖ ❖

Old English glass was installed in the Chapel in the Wood, but the tomb of Capoccio, intended for the Chapel, was found to be too large when it arrived and was broken into segments. In the 20th century the glass disappeared from the Chapel and reappeared in the Bexhill Church from which it was first taken in the 18th century.

"To the Rev. William Cole,   Strawberry Hill, 23 October 1771

..... I am making a very curious purchase at Paris, the complete armour of Francis the First. It is gilt in relief, and is very rich and beautiful. It comes out of the Crozat Collection. I am building a small chapel, too, in my garden, to receive two valuable pieces of antiquity, and which have been presents singularly lucky for me. They are the window from Bexhill with the portraits of Henry III and his Queen, procured for me by Lord Ashburnham. The other, great part of the tomb of Capoccio, mentioned in my *Anecdotes of painting* on the subject of the Confessor's shrine, and sent to me from Rome by Mr. Hamilton, our minister at Naples. It is very extraordinary that I should happen to be master of these curiosities. After next summer, by which time my castle and collection will be complete (for if I buy more I must build another castle for another collection), I propose to form another Catalogue and description, and shall take the liberty to call on you for your assistance. In the mean time there is enough new to divert you at present."

"To Sir Horace Mann,   Strawberry Hill, 18 November 1771
..... I expect a treasure tomorrow, a complete suit of armour of Francis the First, which I have bought out of the Crozat collection. It will make a great figure here at Otranto. Mr. Chute is to come, to welcome the monarch at his landing ....."

He describes below for his cousin, Conway, the accident that befell him on 6th January 1772. This was one of numerous explosions of the gunpowder manufactured and stored on Hounslow Heath; but this was 'the big one'. Three powder mills were set off, one from the other, and it was reported that the shock waves were felt as far away as Gloucester. The saints mentioned were set in painted glass windows, one either side of the front door of Strawberry. In the second world war there was another explosion when a bomb dropped close by, but again the villa suffered no major damage, and it has been suggested that the unusual combination of materials used for building enabled the fabric to give with the tremours rather than to fall.

"To Henry Seymour Conway,   Late Strawberry Hill, 7 January 1772
You have read of my calamity without knowing it, and will pity me when you do. I have been blown up; my castle is blown up; Guy Fawkes has been about my house; and the 5th of November has fallen on the 6th of January! In short, nine thousand powder-mills broke loose yesterday morning on Hounslow-Heath; a whole squadron of them came hither, and have broken eight of my painted-glass windows; and the north side of the castle looks as if it had stood a siege. The two saints in the hall have suffered martyrdom! they have had their bodies cut off, and nothing remains but their heads. The

two next great sufferers are indeed two of the least valuable, being the
passage-windows to the library and great parlour – a fine pane is demolished
in the Round Room; and the window by the Gallery is damaged. Those in
the Cabinet, and Holbein Room, and Gallery, and Blue Room, and Green
Closet, etc., have escaped. As the storm came from the north-west, the China
Closet was not touched, nor a cup fell down. The bow-window of brave old
coloured glass, at Mr. Hindley's is massacred; and all the north sides of
Twickenham and Brentford are shattered. At London it was proclaimed an
earthquake, and half the inhabitants ran into the street.

As Lieutenant-General of the Ordnance, I must beseech you to give
strict orders that no more powder-mills may blow up. My aunt, Mrs.
Kerwood, reading one day in the papers that a distiller's had been burnt by
the head of the still flying off, said she wondered they did not make an act
of parliament against the heads of stills flying off. Now I hold it much
easier for you to do a body this service; and would recommend to your
consideration, whether it would not be prudent to have all magazines of
powder kept under water till they are wanted for service. In the mean time,
I expect a pension to make me amends for what I have suffered under the
government. Adieu!"

As well as visiting France Walpole made frequent journeys around England; in
the next letter he discusses the parks of Clumber and Thoresby, estates belonging to the Dukes of Newcastle and Kingston. His staff were left in charge of
Strawberry Hill, where Margaret Young was housekeeper at this time, and took
visitors over the house. It appears that she was prone to embellish the truth.

"To the Rev. William Mason,   24 August 1772
I should be very ungrateful, dear Sir, after all your goodness to me, particularly
for your kind request in asking an account of my journey, if I did not immediately thank you for all your favours. My journey was as agreeable as it could
be after leaving so pleasant a place and such good company, and was attended
by no accident, except an escape from being drowned in a torrent of whores
and apprentices at Barnet races. I passed through Clumber and Thoresby parks,
and saw no one temptation to stop in either. Strawberry I found parched to the
bone; it has rained for three days since, which has only brought down bushels
of dead leaves, and advanced autumn without its change of hues. To make me
amends, I found my new bedchamber finished, and it is so charming that I
have lost all envy of Castle Howard. The bed would become Cleopatra on the
Cydnus, or Venus if she was not past Cupid-bearing. In truth I fear I must call
it Sardanapalus's, who, Margaret may, without a breach of veracity, assure
strangers lived still longer ago than the Goths ....."

The chest discussed with Mann below he attributed to Benvenuto Cellini. It was intended for the state bedchamber which held a glazed wig cupboard. Although he claims to have finished building, the Beauclerc Tower was to follow, and the New Offices built away from the main house were not completed until 1792; so he had another twenty years of building at Strawberry Hill.

"To Sir Horace Mann,   Strawberry Hill, 29 August 1772
..... How can you speak so slightingly of the fine chest of Benvenuto? It is most beautiful, and fitted up in the prettiest manner: nor do I at all perceive ill usage in it. Mr. Chute, who is here, is delighted with it; and the more, in that the top is copied from a most scarce print after Raphael by Marc Antonio which Stosch procured for him, and which is different from three others. The chest is deposited in a new glazed closet in a sumptuous state bedchamber, which was finished but today, and which completes my house. It must terminate it, for I have at last exhausted all my hoards and collections – and such a quantity of things were scarce ever amassed together! ....."

The niece mentioned in the next letter was the illegitimate daughter of his brother Edward. Her first husband had been the second Earl Waldegrave who died in 1763. She then secretly married the Duke of Gloucester, brother to the King, in 1766. After the eventual acceptance of the marriage by the King Walpole proudly refers to her as "My Royal niece".

"To Sir Horace Mann,   Strawberry Hill, 20 September 1772
There is an end of palliating, suppressing, or disbelieving: the marriage, my niece's marriage, is formally notified to the King by the Duke of Gloucester. Many symptoms had convinced me of late that so it would be. Last Wednesday night I received a letter signed Maria Gloucester, acquainting me that the declaration has been made, and received by his Majesty with grief, tenderness, and justice. I say justice, 'tout oncle' as I am, for it would have been very unjust to the Duke of Cumberland to have made any other distinction between two brothers equally in fault, than what affextion without overt acts cannot help making. This implies that the Duke of Gloucester must undergo the same prohibition as his brother did, which I am told is to be the case, though the step is not yet taken.

    Having acted so rigorously while I could have any doubt of any sort left, it was but decent now to show that respect, nay gratitude, for so great an honour done to the family, which was due to the Prince, and still more to his honour and justice. I accordingly begged the Duchess to ask leave for me to kiss his Royal Highness's hand, which was immediately granted. I went directly to the Pavillions at Hampton Court, where they were, and the Duke received me with great goodness, even drawing an arm-chair for me himself when I refused to continue sitting by the Duchess, or even to sit at all. He entered into the detail of his reasons for declaring the marriage, which he knew, by a former letter to the Duchess, I had approved their not publishing so far as her taking the title; and by something that dropped apropos to the title, I am persuaded that my having obstinately avoided all connection with him, had been a principal cause of his anger, though I do not doubt but some who were averse to the marriage had said everything they could to the disadvantage of the family; and as I had shown most disapprobation of the connexion, impressions against me naturally took the easiest root. Well! here ends my part of this history; I neither shall be, nor seek to be a favourite, and as little a counsellor ....."

The Countess of Upper Ossory had a child by Ossory whilst still married to her first husband, the Duke of Grafton. She was divorced, remarried to Ossory but banished to the country. She became the correspondent to whom Walpole sent news of all that amused him. There is a suggestion in these letters of backstairs gossip, whispers and scandal, and in them Walpole conjures up for her past friends, haunts, activities, amusements and hazards. It is in his letters to her, written towards the end of his life, that we read about his day to day pastimes and excitements.

"To Lady Ossory,   Strawberry Hill, 9 August 1773
..... I wish you joy, Madam, of the sun's settling in England. Was ever such a southern day as this? My house is a bower of tuberoses, and all Twitnam-shire is passing through my meadows to the races at Hampton Court. The picture is incredibly beautiful; but I must quit my joys for my sorrows. My poor Rosette is dying. She relapsed into her fits the last night of my stay at Nuneham, and has suffered exquisitely ever since. You may believe I have too; I have been out of bed twenty times every night, have had no sleep, and sat up with her till three this morning; but I am only making you laugh at me; I cannot help it – I think of nothing else. Without weak-nesses I should not be I, and I may as well tell them as have them tell themselves."

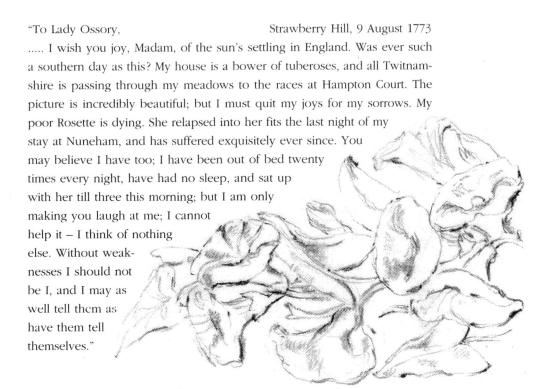

Walpole's greatest friend was John Chute. The serenity and harmony which can be seen in the building of the West Front or the Library of Strawberry Hill are due to Chute's designs. It is his combination of Gothicism with serenity, balanced by imaginative use of detail and freshness of ideas, all laced with heraldic motif, which went a long way towards making Strawberry the 'gingerbread castle' that Walpole loved so much, and gave rise to the epitaph in the following letter with the sadness of the last sentence.

"To Sir Horace Mann,   Strawberry Hill, 27 May 1776
This fatal year puts to the proof the nerves of my friendship! I was disappointed of seeing you when I had set my heart on it; and now I have lost Mr. Chute! It is a heavy blow; but such strokes reconcile one's self to parting with this pretty vision, life! What is it, when one has no longer those to whom one speaks as confidentionally as to one's own soul? Old friends are the great blessing of one's latter years – half a word conveys one's meaning. They have memory of the same events, and have the same mode of thinking. Mr. Chute and I agreed invariably in our principles; he was my counsel in my affairs, was my oracle in taste, the standard to whom I submitted my trifles, and the genius that presided over poor Strawberry! His sense decided me in everything; his wit and quickness illuminated everything. I saw him oftener than any man; to him in every difficulty I had recourse, and him I loved to have here, as our friendship was so entire, and we knew one another so entirely, that he alone never was the least constraint to me. We passed many hours together without saying a syllable to each other; for we were both above ceremony. I left him without excusing myself, read or wrote before him, as if he were not present, Alas! alas! and how self presides even in our grief! I am lamenting myself, not him! – no, I am lamenting my other self. Half is gone; the other remains solitary. Age and sense will make me bear my affliction with submission and composure – but for ever – that little for ever that remains, I shall miss him."

"To Lady Ossory,   [Probably from Strawberry Hill] on 1 June 1776
..... You laugh at my distresses, Madam, but it is a very serious thing to have taken an old cook as yellow as a dishclout, and have her seduced by a jolly dog of a coachman, and have her miscarry of a child and go on with a dropsy, so that she can neither employ him nor I her, nor which is worse, get rid of her. All my servants think that the moment they are useless, I must not part with them, and so I have an infirmary instead of a ménage; and those that are good for anything, do nothing but get children, so that my house is a mixture of a county and foundling hospitals ....."

After Chute's death Walpole looked around for another architect for the New Offices; this building was originally built to house the Strawberry Hill Press, Walpole's horses and servants.

"To the Rev. William Cole,   Strawberry Hill, June 1 1776
..... What is become of Mr. Essex? Does he never visit London? I wish I could tempt him thither or hither. I am not only thinking of building my offices in the collegiate style, for which I have a good design and wish to consult him, but I am actually wanting assistance at this very moment about a smaller gallery that I wish to add this summer; and which if Mr. Essex was here he should build directly. It is scarce worth asking him to take the journey on purpose, though I would pay for his journey hither and back, and would lodge him here for the necessary time. I can only beg you to mention it to him as an idle jaunt, the object is so trifling. I wish more that you could come with him ....."

James Essex, The "Gothic architect from Cambridge" also worked on the hexagonal closet in the Beauclerc Tower built about 1776, which was the last addition to be built onto the main house. It still stands hung with its original Indian blue damask wall covering. The purpose of the tower, with its closet, was to house the seven designs painted in soot water by a semi-professional artist, Lady Diana Beauclerc to illustrate Walpole's play *The Mysterious Mother*. Lady Diana (elsewhere in the letters referred to as Lady Di and Lady Diana Spencer) was a daughter of the Duke of Marlborough; she made an unhappy marriage to Viscount Bolingbroke and had an affair with Topham Beauclerc, a descendant of Charles II and Nell Gwynn. After being divorced by Bolingbroke for adultery in 1768 she married Beauclerc, a man widely famed for the number of fleas inhabiting his person! This marriage too seems to have ended unhappily. She was one of the many women with whom Walpole became friends. The actual quality of her work is difficult to assess; her designs for cameos were used on some pieces of Josiah Wedgwood's wares and it can therefore be assumed that she was reasonably successful, but the putti and cherubs that she favoured are full of an overblown roccoco charm that is not really to 20th century taste.

The play *The Mysterious Mother* is quite extraordinary and was never successful, although dubbed by Byron 'a tragedy of the highest order, and not a puling love-play'. It was regarded at the time as pornographic because its theme was double incest, however the designs for stage sets drawn by Lady Di show lots of bouncing dimpled children and bear little relation to incest or pornography. Set in the Reformation it has a central character of a mother, the

Countess, of Narbonne, who 'stands in' for the girl her son intends to seduce in order to save her virtue, and then attempts sixteen years later to prevent her son marrying the daughter that was the result of their surreptitious union.

✦ ✦ ✦

Whilst the building of the tower was taking place the interior was also being changed, and the Yellow Bedchamber on the ground floor was hung with portraits of court beauties.

"To Lady Ossory,   Arlington Street, 20 June 1776
..... I am to have Mr. Essex tomorrow from Cambridge to try if he can hang me on anywhere another room for Lady Di's drawings. I have turned the little yellow bedchamber below stairs into a beauty room, with the pictures I bought, along with the Cowley, at Mr Lovibond's sale, but I could not place the drawings there, because I will have a sanctuary for them, not to be shown to all the profane that come to see the house, who in truth almost drive me out of my house. Adieu! Madam, remember this is summer, and that I am Methusalem. He left off writing news when he was past an hundred."

"To Henry Seymour Conway,   Strawberry Hill, 30 June 1776
I was very glad to receive your letter, not only because always most glad to hear of you, but because I wished to write to you, and had absolutely nothing to say till I had something to answer. I have lain but two nights in town since

I saw you; have been, else, constantly here, very much employed, though doing, hearing, knowing exactly nothing. I have had a Gothic architect from Cambridge to design me a gallery, which will end in a mouse, that is, in an hexagon closet of seven feet diameter. I have been making a Beauty Room, which was effected by buying two dozen of small copies of Sir Peter Lely, and hanging them up; and I have been making hay, which is not made, because I put it off for three days, as I chose it should adorn the landscape when I was to have company; and so the rain is come, and has drowned it. However, as I can even turn calculator when it is to comfort me for not minding my interest, I have discovered that it is five to one better for me that my hay should be spoiled than not; for, as the cows will eat it if it is damaged, which horses will not, and as I have five cows and but one horse, is not it plain that the worse my hay is the better? ....."

The 18th century was the great period of rebuilding in London when the small central area expanded into large new estates; in particular, the period following the Peace of Paris in 1763 was one of great expansion and became the golden age of Georgian architecture with Chambers and Adam leading a large field. It was also the period of the evolution of the 'professional architect' and Strawberry mirrors what was happening in the country as a whole. The early plans were drawn up by 'gentleman architects' – Walpole, Chute and Bentley, with Robinson who had worked on the Blue Breakfast Room superintending the structural alterations, then Robert Adam both gentleman and professional architect joined the Strawberry Hill list, followed by Essex and later another professional, Wyatt.

Adam revolutionised Georgian taste in England and introduced a totally new concept in design; he loved the use of ornament and frequently worked from the antique, chose detail which appealed to him and made it a pivotal theme in a room or house, which is exactly what Walpole was doing with Gothick. Adam's houses were built to reflect a way of life, to assist in the social cavalcade that was 18th century upper class life; Strawberry too was built to reflect a way of life, although a different one. The two came together in the Round Room at Strawberry which Adam was asked to design as a Drawing Room. Walpole directed Adam to use the Gothic detail of the circular window of Old St. Paul's Cathedral as the source for the ceiling and the tomb of Edward the Confessor in Westminster Abbey for the chimney-piece. On its completion by Adam a delighted Walpole showed it to his guests explaining that it was "Edward the Confessor improved by Mr Adam". The combination of Gothick and Adam's neo-classical detail make it a strange room.

✦✦✦

"To Sir Horace Mann,   Strawberry Hill, 17 July 1776

..... I remember when my father went out of place, and was to return visits, which Ministers are excused from doing, he could not guess where he was, finding himself in so many new streets and squares. This was thirty years ago. They have been building ever since, and one would think had imported two or three capitals. London could put Florence into its fob-pocket; but as they build so slightly, if they did not rebuild, it would be just the reverse of Rome, a vast circumference of city surrounding an area of ruins. As its present progress is chiefly north, and Southwark marches south, the metropolis promises to be as broad as long. Rows of houses shoot out every way like a polypus; and, so great is the rage of building everywhere, that, if I stay here a fortnight, without going to town, I look about to see if no new house is built since I went last. America and France must tell us how long this exuberance of opulence is to last! The East Indies, I believe, will not contribute to it much longer. Babylon and Memphis and Rome, probably, stared at their own downfall. Empires did not use to philosophise, nor thought much but of themselves. Such revolutions are better known now, and we ought to expect them – I do not say we do. This little island will be ridiculously proud some ages hence of its former brave days, and swear its capital was once as big again as Paris, or – what is to be the name of the city that will then give laws to Europe? – perhaps New York or Philadelphia,"

"To the Rev. William Cole,   Strawberry Hill, 9 September 1776

May I trouble you, dear Sir, when you see our friend Mr. Essex, to tell him that the tower is covered in, and that whenever he has nothing to do after this week, I shall be very glad to see him here, if he will only send me a line two or three days beforehand. I have carried this little tower higher than the round one, and it has an exceedingly pretty effect, breaking the long line of the house picturesquely, and looking very ancient, thus. I wish this or anything else could tempt you hither ....."

"To Lady Ossory,   Strawberry Hill, 9 October 1776

..... I am quite alone and wishing myself at Ampthill. I did not think Mr. Essex could have come so malapropos; but it is so difficult to get him, and he has built me a tower so exactly of the fourteenth century, that I did not dare to put him off, lest it should not be ready for furnishing next spring. It is one of those tall thin Flemish towers that are crowned with a roof like an extinguisher, and puts one in mind of that at Thornbury, called Buckingham's Plotting Closet – I hope no Cardinal Wolsey will sit on my skirts for the likeness.

I have lately been lent two delicious large volumes of Queen Elizabeth's jewels, plate, and the New Year's gifts to her: every page of one of them is signed by Lord Burleigh. She had more gold and silver plate than Montezuma, and even of her father's plunder of cathedrals and convents, particularly rich mitres set with jewels, and I don't doubt but she sometimes wore them as head of the Church and fancied herself like Pope Joan. I have extracted some of the articles that are most curious, and here they are:

A looking-glass with the 'steel' of agate – (This shows they had no quicksilvered glass – and she must have looked delightfully fierce in a piece of polished steel) – but this was of agate; and the glass was of berril, and had her mother Anne Boleyn's arms. What a treasure this would be at Strawberry!

A porringer of white purselyn (porcelain) garnished with gold, and a lion at top. (The first porcelain I have read of was in Queen Mary's reign.)

One case of leather painted and gilt with the Duke of Northumberland's (Dudley's) arms, having therein one broad knife, one lesser, two forks and seven small knives, the hafts of all being silver, enamelled with his arms and word (motto).

One standish of mother-of-pearl, garnished with silver gilt, with three boxes for ink, dust (sand) and counters of silver gilt – These were, I suppose, to calculate with, as, I think they still do in the Exchequer.

A gilt font with a cover, having at top a gilt cross chased with antique faces; also the hand (handle) and foot, and with roses and pomegranates (for Henry VIII and Cathcrine of Arragon ; this should be at Ampthill against Lord Gowran's christening) upon the brim, and thereon written, Maria Regina, Veritas Temporis filia.

A ship for frankincense of mother-of-pearl, the foot, garnishment, and cover of silver gilt, having the griffon holding the pillar, and Cardinal Wolsey's arms, and a little spoon of silver gilt in it – You see, Madam, by this and the Duke of Northumberland's knives, that it was charming to be a king or queen in those days, and that all was fish that came to the crown's net – In short, I am exceedingly angry at Messrs Hampden and Pym, that were the cause of all these pretty baubles being melted down.

One standing cup of Flanders making, garnished with pearls, enamelled in divers places, containing in the foot thereof, seven trenchers of silver parcel gilt standing upon the sides (I cannot make out the ichnography of this brave cup), seven forks set with three pearls apiece; at the end, seven knives in a case, of the like work, and one pair of snippers (snuffers) , the hafts of the knives of wood, and the ends silver gilt, with a pearl at the end of each; and in the top four goblets gilt, and three cups of assay (for the taster) gilt, twelve spoons gilt, and the salts garnished with false pearls, and prettily enamelled; and a candlestick having two sockets joined together; and in the top, a clock.

One bed-pan, having the Queen's arms enammelled at the end.

Here was luxury and magnificence and taste! – I have a great mind to print these dear MSS, and another of Anne of Denmark's furniture at Somerset House, which was lent to me lately too. This Majesty's joy was in canopies; she had more than there are chairs now in St James's; and now and then she gave a bed to her lady of the sweet coffers. She had sweet bags enough to hold all the perfumes of Arabia, and a suit of arras with the history of Charles Brandon, and embroidered carpets to lay over cupboards, and fine caparisons of purple velvet richly embroidered all over with silver, made for his Highness's horse to tilt with in Spain at the time of his being there, which his Queen Henrietta Maria, being a good huswife, ordered to be converted into a bed, as she ordered another bed to be translated, says the inventory, into the French fashion. Queen Anne had besides, a cradle-mantle of crimson velvet with a broad gold lace bordered with ermines, and lined with carnation taffety; and pillows laced with gold and silver – but alas, she had only six pair of fine Holland sheets, and thirty pair of ordinary Holland. There remained also three folio pages full of the robes of Henry VIII and a diaper table-cloth, whose borders were of gold needlework, and one dozen of napkins suitable; and a smock very richly wrought with gold, silver and silk – pray, Madam, do you think this was her Majesty's wedding shift? – I will mention nothing more, but a cabinet of ebony inlaid with silver, white ebony (probably, ivory) and gilt, with flowers and beasts; and in the drawers, a comb-case furnished, two gilt cups in the shape of turkeys (as I have three castors like owls), a dresser for the tongue (I suppose, a scraper), and sundry pencils and knitting needles; and another cabinet of cloth of silver, lined with orange-tawny velvet (probably a casket).

Well! considering this solid magnificence, must not all good Christians pray, that when His Majesty has sometime or other conquered America, he will extend his arms to Peru and Mexico, that the Crown may eat off of gold trenchers set with pearls, and that the Queen may have smocks as rough with embroidery as hands can make them, and everything for the bed suitable? So prays her and your Ladyship's poor beadsman."

The fan vaulted ceiling of papier-mâché in Walpole's Long Gallery has as its source the side aisle of the Henry VII chapel in Westminster Abbey, but there are other precedents, and the roof of King's College Chapel, where Walpole was a student, is one of them. Apart from the geometry of the fans the main difference between the Gothic fan vaulting of King's and the roof of the Long Gallery at Strawberry is function; Gothic vaulting had a structural function and Walpole's Gothic(k) was always purely decorative. As a style Gothic had never totally died out in England, and in Cambridge Walpole could well imagine himself living back in time in the period he most admired.

"To the Rev. William Cole, Arlington Street, 22 May 1777
..... I have put together some trifles I promised you, and will beg Mr. Lort to
be the bearer when he goes to Cambridge, if I know of it. At present I have
time for nothing I like. My age and inclination call for retirement: I envied
your happy hermitage, and leisure to follow your inclination. I have always
lived post, and shall not die before I can bait – yet it is not my wish to be
unemployed, could I but choose my occupations. I wish I could think of the
pictures you mention, or had time to see Dr. Glynn and the master of
Emmanuel. I dote on Cambridge, and could like to be often there. The
beauty of King's College Chapel, now it is restored, penetrated me with a
visionary longing to be a monk in it; though my life has been passed in
turbulant scenes, in pleasures – or rather pastimes, and in much fashionable
dissipation; still books, antiquity, and virtu kept hold of a corner of my heart,
and since necessity has forced me of late years to be a man of business, my
disposition tends to be a recluse for what remains – but it will not be my
lot: and though there is some excuse for the young doing what they like, I
doubt an old man should do nothing but what he ought, and I hope doing
one's duty is the best preparation for death. Sitting with one's arms folded
to think about it, is a very lazy way of preparing for it. If Charles V had
resolved to make some amends for his abominable ambition by doing good,
his duty as a King, there would have been infinitely more merit than going
to doze in a convent. One may avoid active guilt in a sequestered life; but
the virtue of it is merely negative, though innocence is beautiful ....."

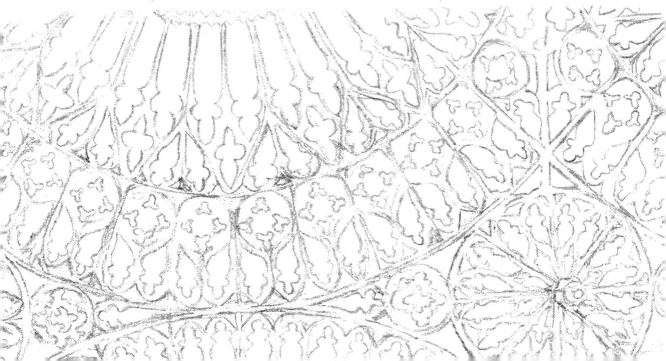

The following letter and the one to Lady Ossory dated 11th August 1778 both refer back to Chatterton's letter to Walpole of 1769, his subsequent death, and the part played in it by Walpole's rejection of his poetry. It seems that detailing the facts helped Walpole to come to terms with Chatterton's death.

Although Walpole steeped himself in Gothic architecture he was not familiar with early English or French literature; had he been it is unlikely that Chatterton would have fooled him; some of the mistakes he made were naive. The following letter is however extremely generous.

"To the Rev. William Cole,   Strawberry Hill, 19 June 1777

..... I did see the 'Monthly Review', but hope one is not guilty of the death of every man who does not make one the dupe of a forgery. I believe M'Pherson's success with 'Ossian' was more the ruin of Chatterton than I. Two years passed between my doubting the authenticity of Rowley's poems and his death. I never knew he had been in London till some time after he had undone and poisoned himself there. The poems he sent me were transcripts in his own hand, and even in that circumstance he told a lie: he said he had them from the very person at Bristol to whom he had given them. If any man was to tell you that monkish rhymes had been dug up at Herculaneum, which was destroyed several centuries before there was any such poetry, should you believe it? Just the reverse is the case of Rowley's pretended poems. They have all the elegance of Waller and Prior, and more than Lord Surrey – but I have no objection to anybody believing what he pleases. I think poor Chatterton was an astonishing genius – but I cannot think that Rowley foresaw metres that were invented long after he was dead, or that our language was more refined at Bristol in the reign of Henry V than it was at Court under Henry VIII. One of the chaplins of the Bishop of Exeter has found a line of Rowley in Hudibras – the monk might foresee that too! The prematurity of Chatterton's genius is, however, full as wonderful, as that such a prodigy as Rowley should never have been heard of till the eighteenth century. The youth and industry of the former are miracles, too, yet still more credible. There is not a symptom in the poems, but the old words, that savours of Rowley's age – change the old words for modern, and the whole construction is of yesterday ....."

When considering the degree of Walpole's responsibility in Chatterton's death, and the truth of his account of the events, the following letter may be taken into consideration although written about a different man; it shows a real generosity of spirit and demonstrates a desire for fairness in his dealings with those below him in rank which would almost certainly have precluded him taking an active role in the Chatterton affair.

"To the Earl of Harcourt,   Strawberry Hill, 18 October 1777

I am sensibly obliged, my dear Lord, by your great goodness, and am most disposed to take the gardener you recommend, if I can. You are so good-natured you will not blame my suspense. I have a gardener that has lived with me above five-and-twenty years; he is incredibly ignorant, and a mule. When I wrote to your Lordship, my patience was worn out, and I resolved at least to have a gardener for flowers. On your not being able to give me one, I half consented to keep my own; not on his amendment, but because he will not leave me, presuming on my long suffering. I have offered him fifteen pounds a year to leave me, and when he pleads that he is old, and that nobody else will take him, I plead that I am old too, and that it is rather hard that I am not to have a few flowers, or a little fruit as long as I live. I shall now try if I can make any compromise with him, for I own I cannot bear to turn him adrift, nor will starve an old servant, though never a good one, to please my nose and mouth. Besides, he is a Scot, and I will not be unjust, even to that odious nation; and the more I dislike him, the less will I allow my partiality to persuade me I am in the right. Every body would not understand this, and the Scotch none of them; but I am sure your Lordship will, and will not be angry that I dally with you. I know how strong my prejudices are, and am always afraid of them ....."

The following letter with its final sentence is ironic in that 1998 is the tercentenary of the building of Chopp'd Straw Hall and both Walpole and his house are as well known now, or even better known, than in the 18th century.

"To Lady Ossory,   Strawberry Hill, 11 August 1778

I had neither room nor time, Madam, to tell you in my last how much I am ashamed to hear the kind things you are so good as to say to me. Very moderate friendship and good-nature would incline one to try and amuse such reasonable grief as yours, especially if letters could effect it, and letters from one that is accustomed to write them, that they cost but the mere half hour. The remnant of an useless life is dedicated to my friends; I have no other employment .....

The next chapter is not so agreeable to me. Contrary to my determination, I have been writing again for the public. I have a horror for the stage of authors, which they call their senilia and which therefore they ought not to write, for what can age produce that is worth showing? My present case is not of choice, but necessity. Somebody has published the poems of Chatterton the Bristol boy, and in the preface intimates that I was the cause of his despair and poisoning himself, and a little more openly is of opinion that I ought to be stoned. This most groundless accusation has driven me to write the whole story – and yet now I have done it in a pamphlet of near thirty pages of larger paper than this, I think I shall not bring myself to publish it. My story is as clear as daylight, I am as innocent as of the death of Julius Caeser, I never saw the lad with my eyes, and he was the victim of his own extravagance two years after all correspondence had ceased between him and me – and yet I hate to be the talk of the town, and am more inclined to bear this aspersion, than to come again upon the stage. I intend to consult every friend I have before I resolve, and of course, Lord Ossory and your Ladyship. It is impossible to have a moment's doubt on the case. The whole foundation of the accusation is reduced to this – if I had been imposed upon, my countenance might have saved the poor lad from poisoning himself for want, which he brought on himself by his excesses. Those few words are a full acquittal, and would indeed be sufficient – but the story in itself is so marvellous, that I could not help going into the whole account of such a prodigy as Chatterton was. You will pity him, as I do; it was a deep tragedy, but interests one chiefly from his extreme youth, for it was his youth that made his talents and achievements so miraculous. I doubt, neither his genius nor his heart would have interested one, had he lived twenty years more. You will be amazed at what he was capable of before eighteen, the period of his existence – yet I had rather anybody else were employed to tell the story.

As I have taken such an aversion to the character of author, I have fallen into a taste that I never had in my life, that of music. The swan, you know, Madam, is drawing towards its end, when it thinks of warbling, but as I have not begun to sing myself, I trust it is but distantly symptomatic. In short, I have only lived with musicians lately and liked them. Mr. Jerningham is here at Twickenham, and sings in charming taste to his harp. My niece Miss Churchill has been here with her harp, and plays ten times better and sings worse – but I am quite enchanted with Mr. Gammon, the Duke of Grafton's brother-in-law. It is the most melodious voice I ever heard; like Mr. Meynell's but more perfect. As I pass a great deal of time at Hampton Court, in a way very like the remnant of the Court of St Germain's (– and I assure you, where there are some that I believe were of that Court), I was strolling in the gardens in the evening with my nieces, who joined Lady Scaub and Lady Fitzroy, and the former asked Mr. Gammon to sing. His taste is equal to his voice, and his deep notes, the part I prefer, are calculated for the solemnity of Purcel's music, and for what I love particularly, his mad songs and the songs of sailors. It was moonlight and late, and very hot, and the lofty facade of the palace, and the trimmed yews and canal, made me fancy myself of a party in Grammont's time

– so you don't wonder that by the help of imagination I never passed an evening more deliciously. When by the aid of some historic vision and local circumstance I can romance myself into pleasure, I know nothing transports me so much. Pray, steal from your soldiery, and try this secret at Bevis Mount and Nettley Abbey. There are Lord Peterborough and Pope to people the scene, and who you please at Nettley – I sometimes dream, that one day or other somebody will stroll about poor Strawberry and talk of Lady Ossory – but alas! I am no poet, and my castle is of paper, and my castle and my attachment and I, shall soon vanish and be forgotten together!"

His nieces were frequent visitors to Strawberry Hill, so too was rosy faced Kitty Clive who lived in Little Strawberry Hill, nicknamed Cliveden, a cottage in the grounds.

"To William Mason,   Strawberry Hill, 11 October 1778
..... Lady Laura will describe to you a most brilliant fête that I gave her and her sisters and cousins last Thursday. People may say what they will, but splendid as it was, I am not of opinion that this festival of nieces was absolutely the most charming show that ever was seen. I believe the entertainment given by the Queen of the Amazons to the King of Mauritania in the Castle of Ice, and the ball made for the Princess of Persia by the Duke of Sparta in the Saloon of Roses were both of them more delightful, especially as the contrast of the sable Africans with the shining whiteness of the Thracian heroines, and the opposition between the nudity of the Lacedemonian generals and the innumerable folds of linen in the drapery of the Persian ladies, must have been more singular than all the marvels in the Castle of Strawberry last Thursday. To be sure the illumination of the Gallery surpassed the Palace of the Sun; and when its fretted ceiling, which you know is richer than the roof of paradise, opened for the descent of Mrs. Clive in the full moon, nothing could be more striking ....."

The lease on Walpole's house in Arlington Street was due to expire in 1781, therefore in October 1779 he bought a house, number 40, in Berkeley Square for the sum of £4,000.

His letter to Cole, written from his new house in 1780, puts forward a suggestion for a high altar in Westminster Abbey, which if it had been acted upon would have produced an extraordinary effect, and would have added Strawberry Gothick fantasy to the pure Gothic of the Abbey.

"To the Rev. William Cole,   Berkeley Square, 5 January 1780
..... Westminster Abbey ..... have a very fine tomb of Anne of Cleve, close to the altar, which they did not know, till I told them whose it was, though her

arms are upon it, and though there is an exact plate of it in Sandford. They might at least have cut out the portraits and removed the tomb to a conspicuous situation – but though this age is grown so antiquarian, it has not gained a grain more of sense in that walk – witness as you instance in Mr. Grose's Legends, and in the Dean and Chapter reburying the crown, robes, and ornament of Edward I, there would surely have been as much piety in preserving them in their treasury, as in consigning them again to decay. I did not know that the salvation of robes and crowns depended on receiving Christian burial. At the same time, the Chapter transgress that Prince's will, like all their ancestors; for he ordered his tomb to be opened every year or two years, and receive a new cerecloth or pall but they boast now of having enclosed him so substantially, that his ashes cannot be violated again.

It was the present Bishop-Dean who showed me the pictures and Anne's tomb, and consulted me on the new altar-piece. I advised him to have a light octangular canopy, like the cross at Chichester, placed over the table or altar itself, which would have given dignity to it, especially if elevated by a flight of steps; and from the side arches of the octagon, I would have had a semicircle of open arches that should have advanced quite to the seats of the prebends, which would have discovered the pictures; and through the octogan itself you would have perceived the shrine of Edward the Confessor, which is much higher than the level of the choir – but men who ask advice, seldom follow it, if you do not happen to light on the same ideas with themselves ....."

❖ ❖ ❖

Cities were continually stretching outward in the later part of the century with increased industry and an influx of cheap labour. Jews from Europe, and Roman Catholics from Ireland, poured into London, their expectations small and ready to accept low wages. This engendered animosity, especially amongst Londoners, and when the government attempted to ease restrictions on Catholics the Protestant mob was easily aroused. Walpole's letters giving an account of the Gordon Riots which followed are among his most exciting and graphic, with eye witness accounts of contemporary events that convey with clarity the smallness of London and the way in which the whole city was effected by the violence of the action.

"To Lady Ossory,   Berkeley Square, 29 January 1780
The weather-cock Marquis has taken his part, or rather his leave, and resigned his key on Thursday. But there was a more extraordinary phenomenon in the closet the same day. Lord George Gordon asked an audience, was admitted, and incontinently began reading his Irish pamphlet, and the King had the patience to hear him do so for above an hour, till it

was so dark that the lecturer could not see. His Majesty then desired to be excused, and said he would finish the piece himself. 'Well!' said the lunatic apostle, 'but you must give me your honour that you will read it out.' The King promised, but was forced to pledge his honour. It puts one in mind of Charles II at Scoon, before his Restoration. It is to be hoped this man is so mad, that it will soon come to perfection, unless my plan is adopted, of shutting up in Bedlam the few persons in this country that remain in their senses. It would be easier and much cheaper than to confine all the delirious ....."

"To Sir Horace Mann,   Strawberry Hill, 5 June 1780

..... I must hurry to the history of the day. The Jack of Leyden of the age, Lord George Gordon, gave notice to the House of Commons last week, that he would, on Friday, bring in the petition of the Protestant Association; and he openly declared to his disciples, that he would not carry it unless a noble army of martyrs, not fewer than forty thousand, would accompany him. Forty thousand, led by such a lamb, were more likely to prove butchers than victims; and so, in good truth, they were very near being. Have you faith enough in me to believe that the sole precaution taken was, that the Cabinet Council on Thursday empowered the First Lord of the Treasury to give proper orders to the civil magistrates to keep the peace, – and his Lordship forgot it!

Early on Friday morning the conservators of the Church of England assembled in St George's Fields to encounter the dragon, the old serpent, and marched in lines of six and six – about thirteen thousand only, as they were computed – with a petition as long as the procession, which the apostle himself presented; but, though he had given out most Christian injunctions for peaceable behaviour, he did everything in his power to promote a massacre. He demanded immediate repeal of toleration, told Lord North he could have him torn to pieces, and, running every minute to the door or windows, bawled to the populace that Lord North would give them no redress, and that now this member, now that, was speaking against them.

In the mean time, the Peers, going to their own Chamber, and as yet not concerned in the petition, were assaulted; many of their glasses were broken, and many of their persons torn out of the carriages. Lord Boston was thrown down and almost trampled to death; and the two Secretaries of State, the Master of the Ordnance, and Lord Willoughby were stripped of their bags or wigs, and the three first came into the House with their hair all dishevelled. The chariots of Sir George Savile and Charles Turner, two leading advocates for the late toleration, though in Opposition, were demolished; and the Duke of Richmond and Burke were denounced to the mob as proper objects for sacrifice. Lord Mahon laboured to pacify the tempest, and towards eight and nine, prevailed on so many to disperse, that the Lords rose and departed in quiet; but every avenue to the other House was beseiged and blockaded, and for four hours they kept their doors locked, though some of the warmest members proposed to sally out, sword in hand, and cut their way. Lord North and that House behaved with great firmness, and would not submit to give any other satisfaction to the rioters, than to consent to take the Popish laws into consideration on the following Tuesday; and, calling the Justices of the Peace, empowered them to call out the whole force of the country to quell the riot.

The magistrates soon brought the Horse and Foot Guards, and the pious ragamuffins soon fled; so little enthusiasm fortunately had inspired them; at least all their religion consisted in outrage and plunder; for the Duke of Northumberland, General Grant, Mr. Mackinsy, and others, had their pockets picked of their watches and snuff-boxes. Happily, not a single life was lost.

This tumult, which was over between nine and ten at night, had scarce ceased before it broke out in two other quarters. Old Haslang's Chapel was broken open and plundered; and, as he is a Prince of Smugglers as well as Bavarian Minister, great quantities of run tea and contraband goods were found in his house. This one cannot lament; and still less, as the old wretch has for these forty years usurped a hired house, and, though the proprietor for many years has offered to remit his arrears of rent he will neither quit the house nor pay for it.

Monsieur Cordon, the Sardinian Minister, suffered still more. The mob forced his chapel, stole two silver lamps, demolished everything else, threw the benches into the street, set them on fire, carried the brands into the chapel, and set fire to that; and, when the engines came, would not suffer them to play till the Guards arrived, and saved the house and probably all that part of the town. Poor Madame Cordon was confined by illness. My cousin, Thomas Walpole, who lives in Lincoln's Inn Fields, went to her rescue, and dragged her, for she could scarce stand with terror and weakness, to his own house.

I doubt this narrative will not re-approach you and Mr. Windham. I have received yours of the 20th of last month.

You will be indignant that such a mad dog as Lord George should not be knocked on the head. Colonel Murray did tell him in the House, that, if any lives were lost, his Lordship should join the number. Nor yet is he so lunatic as to deserve pity. Besides being very debauched, he has more knavery than mission. What will be decided on him, I do not know; every man that heard him can convict him of the worst kind of sedition: but it is dangerous to constitute a rascal a martyr. I trust we have not much holy fury left; I am persuaded that there was far more dissoluteness than enthusiasm in the mob: yet the episode is very disagreeable. I came from town yesterday to avoid the birthday. We have a report here that the Papists last night burnt a Presbyterian meeting-house, but I credit nothing now on the first report. It was said to be intended on Saturday, and the Guards patrolled the streets at night; but it is very likely that Saint George Gordon spread the insinuation himself .....

Thursday, 8th.

I am exceedingly vexed. I sent this letter to Berkeley Square on Tuesday, but by the present confusions my servant did not receive it in time. I came myself yesterday, and found a horrible scene. Lord Mansfield's house was just burnt down, and at night there were shocking disorders. London and Southwark were on fire in six places; but the regular troops quelled the sedition by daybreak, and everything now is quiet. A camp of ten thousand men is formed in Hyde Park, and regiments of horse and foot arrive every hour.

Friday morn., 9th.

All has been quiet to-night. I am going to Strawberry for a little rest ....."

Of the succession of printers working at the Strawberry Hill Press Kirgate remained for the longest period, and after the closure of the press became Walpole's secretary, writing correspondence for him when attacks of gout prevented Walpole doing so himself. The handwriting of the two men is remarkably similar and has caused problems in distinguishing one from the other.

"To the Rev. William Mason,   Strawberry Hill, 9 June, at night, 1780
I have not had a moment's time, or one calm enough, to write you a single line, and now am not only fatigued, but know not where to begin, or how to arrange the thousand things I have in my mind. If I am incoherent, you must excuse it, and accept whatever presents itself.

I could not bear to sit here in shameful selfish philosophy, and hear the million of reports, and know almost all I loved in danger, without sharing it. I went to town on Wednesday, and though the night was the most horrible I ever beheld, I would not take millions not to have been present; and should I have seen the conflagration as I must from these windows, I should have been distracted for my friends.

At nine at night, on notice of fire, I went with the Duchess and her daughters to the top of Gloucester House, and thence beheld the King's Bench, which was a little town, and at a distance the New Prison in flames. At past ten I went to General Conway's: in a moment we were alarmed by the servants, and rushing to the street-door saw through Little Warwick-street such an universal blaze, that I had no doubt the Mews, at least St.

Martin's-lane, was on fire. Mr. Conway ran, and I limped after him, to Charing Cross, but, though seemingly close, it was no nearer than the Fleet Market.

At past twelve I went up to Lord Hertford's: two of his sons came in from the Bridge at Blackfriars, where they had seen the toll-houses plundered and burnt. Instantly arrived their cook, a German Protestant, with a child in his arms, and all we could gather was that the mob was in possession of his house, had burnt his furniture, and had obliged him to abandon his wife and another child. I sent my own footman, for it was only in Woodstock-street, and he soon returned and said it had been only some apprentices who supposed him a Papist on his not illuminating his house, and that three of them and an Irish Catholic Chairman had been secured, but the poor man has lost his all! I drove from one place to another till two, but did not go to bed till between three and four, and ere asleep heard a troop of horse gallop by. My printer, whom I had sent out for intelligence, came not home till past nine the next morning: I feared he was killed, but then I heard of such a scene. He had beheld three sides of the Fleet Market in flames, Barnard's Inn at one end, the prison on one side and the distiller's on the other, besides Fetter and Shoe Lanes, with such horrors of distraction, distress, etc., as are not to be described; besides accounts of slaughter near the Bank. The engines were cut to pieces, and a dozen or fourteen different parts were burning. It is incredible that so few houses and buildings in comparison are in ashes. The papers must tell you other details, and of what preceded the total demolition of Lord Mansfield's, etc.

Yesterday was some slaughter in Fleet-street by the Horseguards, and more in St. George's Fields by the Protestant Association, who fell on the rioters, who appear to have been chiefly apprentices, convicts, and all kinds of desperadoes; for Popery is already out of the question, and plunder all the object. They have exacted sums from many houses to avoid being burnt as Popish. The ringleader Lord George is fled. The Bank, the destruction of all prisons and of the Inns of Court, were the principal aims.

The Magistrates, intimidated by demolition of Fielding's and Justice Hyde's houses, did not dare to act. A general Council was summoned at Buckingham House, at which the twelve Judges attended. It was determined not to shut up the Courts but to order military execution. Both Houses are adjourned to Monday sevennight, which hurt General Conway so much, who intended yesterday to move for the repeal of the Toleration, and found the House adjourned before he could get to it, though early, that he is gone out of town.

The night passed quietly, and by this evening there will be eighteen thousand men in and round the town. As yet there are more persons killed by drinking than by ball or bayonet. At the great Popish distiller's they swallowed spirits of all kinds, and Kirgate saw men and women lying dead in the streets under barrows as he came home yesterday.

We have now, superabundantly, to fear robbery: 300 desperate villains were released from Newgate. Lady Albemarle was robbed at Mrs. Keppel's door in Pall Mall at twelve at night. Baron d'Aguilar's coach was shot at here last night, close to the Crown.

I have so much exerted my no strength, and had so little sleep these two nights, that I came hither to-day for some rest. It will be but grim repose. It is said that this insurrection was expected in France a month ago. Just as I came away Mr. Griffith told me the French were embarking. In short, what may not be expected? Then one turns from what is to come, to helpless misery, that will soon be forgotten but by the sufferers; whole families ruined, wives that tried to drag their husbands out of the mobs and have found them breathless, the terrors of the Catholics, indeed of all foreigners, but one ....."

❖ ❖ ❖

Walpole met Madame du Deffand in Paris and regularly visited her when in France. Their friendship became one of the strangest episodes of his life. She was twenty years his senior, blind, autocratic, a past royal mistress, and expected Walpole's allegiance. She gave him friendship and her love, demanding his in return. He considered her friendship did him great honour, enjoyed her wit; they wrote over 800 letters to each other over a period of fourteen years, but on his instructions his letters to her were returned to him and destroyed after his death, few survive, and it is difficult to measure his exact feelings for her. He travelled to France four times to visit her, refused money from her, but accepted her bad tempered black spaniel on her death. Tonton was not house trained and bit friends and foes alike; he was brought to Strawberry Hill where he immediately made himself at home and caused chaos. Together with the bequest to Horace of her dog she also left him a gold snuff box with Tonton's portrait on the lid sitting alert with paw upraised.

"To Sir Horace Mann,   Strawberry Hill, 9 October 1780
Since I wrote ..... I heard from Paris of the death of my dear old friend Madame du Deffand, whom I went so often thither to see. It was not quite unexpected, and was softened by her great age, eighty-four, which forbad distant hopes, and, by what I dreaded more than her death, her increasing deafness, which, had it become, like her blindness, total, would have been living after death. Her memory only began to impair; her amazing sense and

quickness, not at all. I have written to her once a week for these last fifteen years, as correspondence and conversation could be her only pleasures. You see that I am the most faithful letter-writer in the world – and, alas! never see those I am so constant to! One is forbidden common-place reflections on these misfortunes, because they are commonplace; but is not that because they are natural? But you never having known that dear old woman is a better reason for not making you the butt of my concern ....."

The plates discussed with Cole were included in the 1784 edition of the *Description* and record areas of the house as Walpole wanted them to be seen, not necessarily as they were.

"To William Cole,   Berkeley Square, 19 December 1780
..... I have two or three plates of Strawberry more than those you mention, but my collections are so numerous, and from various causes, my prints have been in such confusion, that at present I neither know where the plates or proofs are. I intend next summer to set about completing my plan of the *Catalogue* and its prints: and when I have found any of the plates or proofs, you shall certainly have those you want. There are the two large views of the house, one of the cottage, one of the library, one of the front of the road, and the chimney-piece in the Holbein Room I think there are all that are finished – oh! yes, and I believe, the Prior's Garden, but I have not seen them these two years. I was so ill the summer before last, that I attended to nothing; the little I thought of in that way last summer, was to get out my last volumn of the *Anecdotes* – now I have nothing to trouble myself about as an editor, and that not publicly, but to finish my *Catalogue* – and that will be awkwardly enough, for so many articles have been added to my collection since the *Description* was made, that I must add them in the appendix, or reprint it – and what is more inconvenient, the positions of many of the pictures have been changed; so it will be a lame piece of work. Adieu, my dear Sir,
    Yours most cordially,
                       H.W."

When Walpole started to write *The Castle of Otranto* his intention was to make the language colloquial and part of everyday life, although it is far removed from the relaxed style he used in his letters. He had no time for Dr. Johnson, either as a writer or as a man, possibly partly because Johnson disliked Gray's poetry, and Gray was one of Walpole's friends. Pope, criticised here by Johnson, was also one of the writers most admired by Walpole who owned Pope's personal copy of Homer which he had used whilst completing his translation.

"To the Rev. William Mason,   Strawberry Hill, 14 April 1781
..... Sir Joshua Reynolds has lent me Dr. Johnson's 'Life of Pope', which Sir
Joshua holds to be a 'chef-d'-oeuvre'. It is a most trumpery performance, and
stuffed with all his crabbed phrases and vulgarisms, and much trash as anecdotes; you shall judge yourself. He says that all he can discover of Pope's
correspondent, Mr. Cromwell, is that he used to hunt in a tie-wig. The 'Elegy
on the Unfortunate Lady', he says, 'signifies the amorous fury of a raving girl';
and yet he admires the subject of 'Eloisa's Epistle to Abelard'. The machinery
in 'The Rape of Lock', he calls 'combinations of skilful genius with happy
casuality,' in English I guess a 'lucky thought': publishing proposals is turned
into 'emitting' them. But the 66th page is still more curious: it contains a
philosophic solution of Pope's not transcribing the whole 'Iliad' as soon as
he thought he should, and it concludes with this piece of bombast nonsense,
'he that runs against time has an antagonist not subject to casualties'. Pope's
house here he calls 'the house to which his residence afterwards procured
so much celebration,' and that 'his vanity produced a grotto where necessity
enforced a passage'; and that 'of his intellectual character, the constituent
and fundamental principle was good sense, a prompt and intuitive perception
of consonance and propriety.' Was poor good sense ever so unmercifully
overlaid by a babbling old woman? How was it possible to marshal words so
ridiculously? He seems to have read the ancients with no view but of pilfer-
ing polysyllables, utterly insensible to the graces of their simplicity, and these
are called standards of biography! I forgot, he calls Lord Hervey's challenging
Pulteney, 'summoning him to a duel.' Hurlothrumbo talked plain English in
comparison of this wight on stilts, but I doubt I have wearied you ....."

"To Henry Seymour Conway,   Strawberry Hill, Sunday evening, 6 May 1781
..... I told you in my last that Tonton was arrived. I brought him this morning
to take possession of his new villa, but his inauguration has not been
at all pacific. As he has already found out that he may be as despotic
as at Saint Joseph's, he began with exiling my beautiful little cat;
upon which, however, we shall not quite agree. He then flew at one
of my dogs, who returned it by biting his foot till it bled, but was
severely beaten for it. I immediately rung for Margaret to dress his
foot; but in the midst of my tribulation could not keep my countenance; for she cried, 'Poor little thing, he does not understand my
language!' I hope she will not recollect, too, that he is a Papist!"

He had discussed the change of Yellow Bedchamber to Beauty Room with
Lady Ossory in the letter of 20 June 1776. In reminding her of the change five
years later his tone is acerbic.

"To Lady Ossory,   Strawberry Hill, 13 June 1781
The Beauty Room, Madam, is the Yellow Bedchamber hung with Jarvis's
small copies of Sir Peter Lely's beauties, which chamber is on the ground
floor here next to the Little Parlour. I placed your screen there 'pour cause',
and because it accords with the chimney-piece, which is black and yellow.
Had it inhabited the Blue Room in which I chiefly live, it would not have
lasted even my time ....."

"To Lady Ossory,   Strawberry Hill 7 October 1781
..... The night I had the honour of writing to your Ladyship last, I was robbed
– and, as if I were a sovereign or a nation, have had a discussion ever since
whether it was not a neighbour who robbed me ..... Lady Browne and I
were, as usual, going to the Duchess of Montrose at seven o' clock. The
evening was very dark. In the close lane under her park-pale, and within
twenty yards of the gate, a black figure on horseback pushed by between
the chaise and the hedge on my side. I suspected it was a highwayman, and
so I found did Lady Browne, for she was speaking and stopped. To divert
her fears, I was just going to say, Is not that the apothecary going to the
Duchess? when I heard a voice cry 'Stop!' and the figure came back to the
chaise. I had the presence of mind, before I let down the glass, to take out
my watch and stuff it within my waistcoat under my arm. He said, 'Your
purses and watches!' I replied, "I have no watch." 'Then your purse!' I gave
it to him; it had nine guineas. It was so dark that I could not see his hand,
but felt him take it. He then asked for Lady Browne's purse, and said, 'Don't
be frightened; I will not hurt you.' I said, "No; you won't frighten the lady?"
He replied, 'No; I give you my word I will do you no hurt.' Lady Browne
gave him her purse, and was going to add her watch, but he said, 'I am
much obliged to you! I wish you good night!' pulled off his hat, and rode
away. "Well," said I, "Lady Browne, you will not be afraid of being robbed
another time, for you see there is nothing in it." 'Oh! but I am,' said she,
'and now I am in terrors lest he should return, for I have given him a purse
with only bad money that I carry on purpose' ....."

*W*alpole's importance today is summed up in the following letter. For eighty years he was present to see, participate in and comment on the great events of the day, and to meet and know those people who formed Georgian politics and society.

"To Sir Horace Mann,   Berkeley Square, 25 February 1782
..... How strange are the accidents of life! At ten years old I had set my heart on seeing George I, and, being a favourite child, my mother asked leave for me to be presented to him; which to the First Minister's wife was granted, and I was carried by the late Lady Chesterfield to kiss his hand as he went to supper in the Duchess of Kendal's apartment. This was the night but one before he left England the last time; and now, fifty years afterwards, one of his great-grandsons and one of his great-granddaughters are my great-nephew and niece! Yet how little had the first part to do with bringing about the second! When one considers these events abstractedly, as I do, the reflection is amusing; it makes the politician's arts trifling and ridiculous: no plan, no foresight, no industry could have ranged or accomplished what mere chance has effected. It would not be less entertaining, if a politician would talk as frankly on the projects he had planned and been disappointed of effecting; but a politician would not look on the dénouement with the same indifference."

Walpole enjoyed coining new words: serendipity is one, gloomth another. Gloomth describes the darkness of Strawberry Hill mixed with warmth which was present in the public space of the house. The next letter conjures up brilliantly the atmosphere he had striven to create.

"To Lady Ossory,   Berkeley Square, 20 June 1783
..... The month of June has been as abominable as any one of its ancestors in all the pedigree of the Junes. I was literally half drowned on Sunday night. it rained through two stories and into the Green Closet at Strawberry, and my bedchamber was wet to its smock. The gutters were stopped or could not carry off the deluge fast enough. Margaret prayed to St Rainbow, but as he never appears till it is too late, we were forced to have recourse to mortal help and litter all the floors with hay to soak up the inundation.
     I had a worse woe the next night. The house of De Guines had notified to Lady Ailesbury their intention of visiting Strawberry, and she had proposed to bring them to breakfast. At first I refused, but reflecting that they might invade me unawares like the Duc de Chartres, I had agreed that she should bring them yesterday – but lo! on Monday morning Lady Pembroke wrote to me that she would bring them to drink tea that evening. I told her

my arrangement, but left it to her option to do as she pleased. From dinner-time I sat at the window watching for them, and taking every old woman with a basket on her head for a coach and six. It rained all the time as it had done the preceeding evening. At last, at half an hour after seven, as I had left it to their option, and the night was so bad and dark, I concluded they had given it up, and called for my tea – but alas! at a quarter before eight the bell rang at the gate – and behold a procession of the Duke, his two daughters, the French ambassador (on whom I had meant to sink myself), Lady Pembroke, Lord Herbert and Lord Robert. The first word M. de Guines said was to beg I would show them all I could – Imagine, Madam, what I could show them when it was pitch dark! Of all houses upon earth mine, from the painted glass and overhanging trees, wants the sun the most, besides the Star Chamber and passage being obscured on purpose to raise the gallery. They ran their foreheads against Henry VII and took the grated door of the Tribune for the dungeon of the castle. I mustered all the candlesticks in the house, but before they could be lighted up, the young ladies, who by the way are extremely natural, agreeable and civil, were seized with a panic of highwaymen and wanted to go. I laughed and said, I believed there was no danger, for that I had not been robbed these two years. However, I was not quite in the right; they were stopped in Knightsbridge by two footpads, but Lady Pembroke having lent them a servant besides their own unique, they escaped – and so much for the French and the rain – I wish the latter were as near going as the former ....."

"To Henry Seymour Conway,   Strawberry Hill, 27 July 1783
..... I can give you but an indifferent account of myself. I went to Lord Dacre's but whether the heat and fatigue were too much for me, or whether the thunder turned me sour, for I am at least as weak as small beer, I came back with the gout in my left hand and right foot. The latter confined me for three days; but though my ankle is still swelled, I do not stay in my house – however I am frightened and shall venture no more expeditions yet, for my hands and feet are both so lame that I am neither comfortable to myself or anybody else, abroad, when I must confine them, stay by myself, or risk pain, which the least fatigue gives me .....

I know nothing upon earth but my own disasters. Another is, that all yesterday I thought all my gold-fish stolen. I am not sure that they are not; but they tell me they keep at the bottom of the water from the hot weather. It is all to be laded out tomorrow morning and then I shall know whether they are gone or boiled .....

As I was rising this morning, I received an express from your daughter that she will bring Madame de Cambis and Lady Melbourne to dinner here tomorrow. I shall be vastly pleased with the party – but it puts Philip and Margaret to their wit's end to get them a dinner – nothing is to be had here; we must send to Richmond and Kingston and Brentford; I must borrow Mr Ellis's cook, and somebody's confectioner and beg somebody's fruit, for I have none of these of my own nor know anything of the matter – but that is Philip and Margaret's affair and not mine, and the worse the dinner is, the more Gothic Madame de Cambis will think it ....."

The house became a great tourist attraction and Walpole issued tickets for visitors, the Strawberry Hill Press printing instructions on how to apply for them, which appears to have had the effect of increasing the popularity of the tickets and of publicising the house. Margaret, Walpole's housekeeper, took those visitors around Strawberry Hill who had received tickets; four visitors were admitted on one ticket each day during the summer months as long as they did not arrive on the wrong day, or the wrong time, or with their children! It became the convention for each member of the party to tip her a guinea – an enormous sum at a time when a housekeeper would have earned between twenty and fifty pounds a year. This letter is written very tongue-in-cheek.

"To Lady Ossory,   Strawberry Hill, 4 August 1783
..... A propos to matrimony, I want to consult your ladyship very seriously: I am so tormented by droves of people coming to see my house, and Margaret gets such sums of money by showing it, that I have a mind to marry her, and so repay myself that way for what I have flung away to make my house quite uncomfortable to me. I am sure Lord Denbigh would have proposed to her had he known of her riches; and I doubt Margaret could not have resisted the temptation of being a Countess more than Lady Holford. She certainly can never have a more disagreeable suitor: and therefore I grow every day more in danger of losing her and all her wealth. Mr. Williams said this morning that Margaret's is the best place in England, and wondered Mr. Gilbert did not insist on knowing what it is worth. Thank my stars, he did not! Colonel Barré or Lord Ashburton would propose to suppress housekeepers and then humbly offer to show my house themselves, and the first would calculate what he had missed by not having shown it for the last ten years, and expect to be indemnified; for virtue knows to a farthing what it has lost by not having been vice. Good night, Madam; my poor rheumatic shoulder must go to bed."

On the death of his brother Walpole's nephew George inherited the title and became 3rd Earl of Orford. George was a gambler and suffered from periods of insanity during which times his uncle administered the Orford estates very ably. George is chiefly remembered today for a race he organised from Norfolk to London between five geese and five turkeys, and for making necessary the sale of Sir Robert's picture collection to Catherine the Great.

"To Lady Ossory,   Strawberry Hill, 19 June 1784
..... Captain Cook's 'Voyage' I have neither read nor intend to read. I have seen the prints – a parcel of ugly faces, with blubber lips and flat noses, dressed as unbecomingly as if both sexes were ladies of the first fashion; and rows of savages, with backgrounds of palm-trees. Indeed I shall not give five guineas and a half – nay, they sell already for nine, for such uncouth lubbers; nor do I desire to know how unpolished the north or south poles have remained ever since Adam and Eve were just such mortals. My brother's death has made me poor, and I cannot now afford to buy everything I see. It is late, to be sure, to learn economy, but I must do it, though a little grievous, as I never was able to say the multiplication table ....."

Balloons became enormously popular, fascinated Walpole and became the subject of satire. W. S. Lewis noted that the Print Room of the Lewis Walpole Library at Farmington owned twenty five satiric prints of 1784 on the subject of balloons and ballooning.

"To Henry Seymour Conway,   Strawberry Hill, 30 June 1784
..... I have, at last, seen an air-balloon; just as I once did see a tiny review, by passing one accidentally on Hounslow-heath. I was going last night to Lady Onslow at Richmond, and over Mr. Cambridge's field I saw a bundle in the air not bigger than the moon, and she herself could not have descended with more composure if she had expected to find Endymion fast asleep. It seemed to light on Richmond-hill; but Mrs. Hobart was going by, and her coiffure prevented my seeing it alight. The papers say, that a balloon has been made at Paris representing the castle of Stockholm, in compliment to the King of Sweden; but that they are afraid to let it off: so, I suppose, it will be served up to him in a dessert. No great progress, surely, is made in these airy navigations, if they are still afraid of risking the necks of two or three subjects for the entertainment of a visiting sovereign. There is seldom a 'feu de joie' for the birth of a Dauphin that does not cost more lives. I thought royalty and science never haggled about the value of blood when experiments are in the question.

I shall wait for summer before I make you a visit. Though I dare to say that you have converted your smoke-kilns into a manufacture of balloons, pray do not erect a Strawberry castle in the air for my reception, if it will cost a pismire a hair of its head. Good night! I have ordered my bed to be heated as hot as an oven, and Tonton and I must go into it."

"To Sir Horace Mann,   [Probably from Berkeley Square in February 1785] ..... I sometimes think I have lived two or three lives. My thirteen months at Florence was a pleasant youth to one of them. Seven months and a half at Paris, with four or five journeys thither since, was a middle age, quite different from five-and-twenty years in Parliament which had preceeded – and an age since! Besides, as I was an infant when my father became Minister, I came into the world at five years old; knew half the remaining Courts of King William and Queen Anne, or heard them talked of as fresh; being the youngest and favourite child, was carried to almost the first operas, kissed the hand of George the First, and am now hearing the frolics of his great-great-grandson; – no, all this cannot have happened in one life! I have seen a mistress of James II, the Duke of Marlborough's burial, three or four wars, the whole career, victories and death of Lord Chatham, the loss of America, the second conflagration of London by Lord George Gordon – and yet I am not so old as Methusalem by four or five centuries ....."

"To Sir Horace Mann,   Berkeley Square, 24 June 1785 ..... On reading over your Florentine gazette, I observed that the Great Duke has a manufacture of porcelain. If any of it is sold, I should be glad if your nephew would bring me a single bit, a cup, or other trifle, as a sample. I remember that ages ago there was a manufacture at Florence belonging to Marquis Ginori, of which I wished for a piece, but could not procure one: the grand-ducal may be more obtainable. I have a closet furnished with specimens of porcelain of various countries; besides a good deal of faience or Raphael-ware, and some pieces with the arms of Medici – but am not I an old simpleton to be wanting playthings still? – and how like is one's last cradle to one's first! adieu!

P.S. 28th

Notwithstanding Pilatrier's miscarriage, balloonation holds up its head. Colonel Fitzpatric, Lord Ossory's brother, has ascended in one from Oxford, and was alone. Sadler, whom I thought lost, is come to light again, and was to have been of the voyage, but the vessel not being potent enough for two, the Colonel went alone, had a brush with a high hill in his descent, but landed safe about fifteen miles from the University – how posterity will laugh at us, one way or other! if half a dozen break their necks and balloonism is exploded, we shall be called fools for having imagined it could be brought to use – if it should be turned to account, we shall be ridiculed for having doubted."

Although in the following letter Walpole grumbles about his visitors he continued to issue tickets and to publicise the way in which they could be obtained; he loved showing off his house and his Collection as if it was a museum or a piece of theatre. For special guests he wrote commemorative verses which were printed at the Strawberry Hill Press.

"To Henry Seymour Conway,   Strawberry Hill, 18 June 1786, Sunday night I suppose you have been swearing at the east wind for parching your verdure, and are now weeping for the rain that drowns your hay. I have these calamities in common, and my constant and particular one, – people that come to see my house, which unfortunately is more in request than ever. Already I have had twenty-eight sets, have five more tickets given out; and yesterday, before I had dined, three German barons came. My house is a torment, not a comfort! I was sent for again to dine at Gunnersbury on Friday, and was forced to send to town for a dress-coat and a sword. There were the Prince of Wales, the Prince of Mecklenburg, the Duke of Portland, Lord Clanbrassil, Lord and Lady Clermont, Lord and Lady Southhampton, Lord Pelham, and Mrs. Howe. The Prince of Mecklenburg went back to Windsor after coffee; and the Prince and Lord and Lady Clermont to town after tea, to hear some new French players at Lady William Gordon's. The Princess, Lady Barrymore, and the rest of us, played three pools at commerce till ten. I am afraid I was tired and gaped. While we were at the dairy, the Princess insisted on my making some verses on Gunnersbury. I pleaded being superannuated. she would not excuse me. I promised she should have an Ode on her next Birthday, which diverted the Prince; but all would not do. So, as I came home, I made the following stanzas, and sent them to her breakfast next morning:–

I

In deathless odes for ever green
Augustus' laurels blow;
Nor e'er was grateful duty seen
In warmer strains to flow.

II

Oh! why is Flaccus not alive,
Your favourite scene to sing?
To Gunnersbury's charms could give
His lyre immortal spring.

III

As warm as his my zeal for you,
Great princess! could I show it:
But though you have a Horace too –
Ah, Madame! he's no poet.

If they are but poor verses, consider I am sixty-nine, was half asleep, and
made them almost extempore – and by command! However, they succeeded,
and I received this gracious answer:–

'I wish I had a name that could answer your pretty verses. Your
yawning yesterday opened your vein for pleasing me; and I return you my
thanks, my good Mr. Walpole, and remain sincerely your friend,

Amelia'

I think this is very genteel at seventy-five ....."

Walpole worried about breakages from visitors to the house, but the 'lofty vase'
in which Selima had drowned was kept safe and is still in existence today.

"To Lady Ossory,   Strawberry Hill, 2 August 1786
..... The Vase for which your ladyship is so good as to interest yourself, was
not the famous Cat's 'lofty vase', nor none of any consequence, but a vase
and dish of Florentine Fayence, that stood under the table in the Round
Chamber; nor had I the least concern but for the company who were so
grieved at the accident. With the troops that come, I am amazed I have not
worse damage; however, I am sometimes diverted too. Last week a
scientific lady was here, and exactly at the moment I opened the cabinet of
enamels, she turned to a gentleman who came with her, and entered into a
discussion of the ides and calends. Another gentlewoman was here two days
ago, who has seen a good half century: she said, 'Well I must live another
forty years to have time to see all the curiosities of this house'. These little
incidents of character do not make me amends for being the master of a
puppet-show, for although I generally keep behind the scenes, I am almost
as much disturbed as if I constantly exhibited myself – and

'E'en Sunday shines no Sabbath day to me!'

P.S. – I am told that this has been a fine summer – and in one respect I allow it, for it has brought the winter so forward already, that my grate was in full blow on Monday night with a good fire!"

❖ ❖ ❖

Japanning was highly fashionable, and in 1772 Henry Clay, a Birmingham manufacturer, patented his invention for making furniture, sections of boats and ships, and even carriage panels from lacquered paper. Walpole ordered and owned furniture made by him. Clay's process involved pasting together strips of fabric based paper which were then used as wood, cut, carved, gilded and lacquered. It is likely that the prints used in the next letter would have been printed onto a fabric based paper.

"To Lady Ossory,   Strawberry Hill, 30 August 1786
..... Letters, I know, can be made of lies, as well as newspapers; and we have large manufactures at Richmond and Hampton Court wrought by old ladies themselves, as they used to make japan, by cutting prints to pieces and daubing them over with colours and varnish ....."

❖ ❖ ❖

Walpole updated the *Description* of the house regularly although the last published edition was printed in 1784. In 1800, nine years after his death, J. Scatcherd published the 'Ambulator or A Pocket Companion in a Tour Round London, within the Circuit of Twenty-five miles:' It describes 'whatever is most remarkable for Antiquity, Grandeur, Elegance, or Rural Beauty: including New Catalogues of Pictures; and illustrated by Historical and Biographical Observations; to which are prefixed, a Consise Description of the Metropolis'. It includes a section on Strawberry Hill.

The room-by-room description of Strawberry is fascinating because although large sections of it are lifted straight from Walpole's *Description* other areas of the house are seen with a new eye, and elements that Walpole failed to note, because presumably he thought them unimportant or took them for granted, are noted by the 'Ambulator'. From it we learn of gilding on the chimney-pieces in the Round Room and the Great North Bedchamber, and that the canopy of the bed in the Holbein Chamber was 'crowned with a plume of red and white ostrich feathers. By the side of the bed hangs the red hat of Cardinal Wolsey'. Walpole had described the feathers as purple and white.

The choice of items recorded in 1800 and the style used marks the entry into the Romantic Period. 'The approach to the house, through a grove of lofty trees; the embattled wall, overgrown with ivy; the spiry pinnacles, and gloomy cast of the buildings; give it the air of an ancient abbey, and fill the beholder with awe'.

Walpole would have been greatly pleased by the tone of reporting and by the fact that trees and ivy had at last grown to a respectable Gothic size; he had long bemoaned the slow rate of growth in his garden.

The 'Ambulator' account also enables us to see the house in a period of transition. On his death Walpole bequeathed it, for her lifetime, to Anne Seymour Damer, his cousin Conway's daughter, a favourite of his who had stayed in the house with him several times as a child whilst her parents were abroad. Her portrait, by Cosway, was in Walpole's Collection. She became a well known sculptress of the period, and during her occupancy filled the house with examples of her work. In the Little Parlour stood "Mrs. Damer's much admired model of two dogs in terra cotta" and in the Library "an ofsprey eagle in terra cotta, by Mrs. Damer" – this last was one of Walpole's most cherished items and he described it as being "taken in a rage". She moved articles from the Collection around, a practice started by Walpole who was always changing the position of favourite objects. An account such as that in the 'Ambulator' places the house back in the position of a home and helps to remove the image of a museum which it had acquired at the time of Walpole's death.

"To Lady Ossory,   Strawberry Hill, 15 September 1787
..... the *Description* of this place; now, though printed, I have entirely kept up, and mean to do so while I live for very sound reasons, Madam, as you will allow. I am so tormented by visitors to my house, that two or three rooms are not shown to abridge their stay. In the *Description* are specified all the enamels and minatures, etc., which I keep under lock and key. If the visitors got the book into their hands, I should never get them out of the house, and they would want to see fifty articles which I do not choose they should handle and paw ....."

❖❖❖

In 1787 Walpole first met the Berry family; he was seventy and the two daughters, Mary and Agnes, both in their early twenties, completely transformed his life. Only two years after the first meeting he gave them Little Strawberry Hill to live in, a cottage on his estate which had earlier housed Kitty Clive. Although he was fond of both sisters and called them "his wives", Mary was his favourite because she had the quicker and brighter wit.

"To Lady Ossory,   Strawberry Hill, 11 October 1788
..... I have made a much more, to me, precious acquisition. It is the acquaintance of two young ladies of the name of Berry, whom I first saw last

winter, and who accidentally took a house here with their father for this season. Their story is singular enough to entertain you. The grandfather, a Scot, had a large estate in his own country, 5000 pounds a year it is said; and a circumstance I shall tell you makes it probable. The eldest son married for love a woman with no fortune. The old man was enraged and would not see him. The wife died and left these two young ladies. Their grandfather wished for an heir male, and pressed the widower to re-marry, but could not prevail; the son declaring he would consecrate himself to his daughters and their education. The old man did not break with him again, but much worse, totally disinherited him, and left all to his second son, who very handsomely gave up 800 pounds a year to his elder brother. Mr. Berry has since carried his daughters for two or three years to France and Italy, and they are returned the best-informed and the most perfect creatures I ever saw at their age. They are exceedingly sensible, entirely natural and unaffected, frank, and, being qualified to talk on any subject, nothing is so easy and agreeable as their conversation – not more apposite than their answers and observations. The eldest, I discovered by chance, understands Latin and is a perfect Frenchwoman in her language. The younger draws charmingly, and has copied admirably Lady Di's gipsies, which I lent, though for the first time of her attempting colours. They are of pleasing figures; Mary, the eldest, sweet, with fine dark eyes, that are very lively when she speaks, with a symmetry of face that is the more interesting from being pale; Agnes, the younger, has an agreeable sensible countenance, hardly to be called handsome, but almost. She is less animated than Mary, but seems, out of deference to her sister, to speak seldomer, for they dote on each other, and Mary is always praising her sister's talents. I must even tell you they dress within the bounds of fashion, though fashionably; but without the excrescences and balconies with which modern hoydens overwhelm and barricade their persons. In short, good sense, information, simplicity, and ease characterise the Berrys; and this is not particularly mine, who am apt to be prejudiced, but the universal voice of all who know them. The first night I met them I would not be acquainted with them, having heard so much in their praise that I concluded they would be all pretension. The second time, in a very small company, I sat next to Mary, and found her an angel both inside and out. Now I do not know which I like best, except Mary's face, which is formed for a sentimental novel, but is ten times fitter for a fifty times better thing, genteel comedy. This delightful family comes to me almost every Sunday evening, as our region is too proclamatory to play at cards on the seventh day. I do not care a straw for cards, but I do disapprove of this partiality to the youngest child of the week; while the other poor six days are treated as if they had no souls to save. I forgot to tell you that Mr. Berry is a little man with a round face, and you would not suspect him of so much feeling and attachment. I make no excuse for such minute details ....."

In cleaning and conservation work carried out on the Chapel in the Wood in 1997 a plaque was uncovered on an exterior wall. It is very probable that it marks the spot where Walpole buried his beloved dogs.

"To Lady Ossory,   Berkeley Square, 24 February 1789
..... I ..... delayed telling you that Tonton is dead – and that I comfort myself: he was grown stone deaf, and very near equally blind, and so weak that the two last days he could not walk upstairs. Happily he had not suffered, and died close by my side without a pang or a groan. I have had the satisfaction for my dear old friend's sake and his own, of having nursed him up by constant attention to the age of sixteen, yet always afraid of his surviving me, as it was scarce possible he could meet a third person who would study his happiness equally. I sent him to Strawberry and went thither on Sunday to see him buried behind the Chapel near Rosette. I shall miss him greatly – and must not have another dog – I am too old, and should only breed it up to be unhappy, when I am gone! My resource is in two marble kittens that Mrs Damer has given me of her own work, and which are so much alive that I talk to them as I did to poor Tonton! – if this is being superannuated, no matter; when dotage can amuse itself, it ceases to be an evil. I fear, my marble playfellows are better adapted to me, than I am to being your Ladyship's correspondent! ....."

The friendship of the Berry sisters reawoke emotions and interests which had remained dormant for many years; the change can be seen in the style of his letters to them.

In his last years illness brought delusions and he believed himself abandoned by the sisters; he may never have fully recovered from a fit of jealousy aroused at the proposed, but unfulfilled, marriage of Mary. On his death he left them the use of Little Strawberry Hill for their lifetime, together with £400 each. They chose not to remain there, but Mary Berry arranged for the publication of material Walpole wanted to be read after his death and she defended him against an attack by Macaulay.

"To Miss Berry,   Strawberry Hill, 9 July 1789
..... One would think that it was I was grown young again, for just now, as I was reading your letter in my bedchamber, while some of my customers

are seeing the house, I heard a gentleman in the Armoury ask the housekeeper as he looked at the bows and arrows, 'Pray does Mr Walpole shoot?' .....

..... I wish I had preserved any correspondence in France, as you are curious about their present history; which I believe very momentous indeed. What little I have accidentally heard, I will relate, and will learn what more I can. On the King's being advised to put out his talons, Necker desired leave to resign, as not having been consulted, and as the measure violated his plan. The people, hearing his intention, thronged to Versailles; and he was forced to assure them from a balcony, that he was not to retire. I am not accurate in dates, nor warrant my intelligence, and therefore pretend only to send you detached scraps. Force being still in request, the Duc de Châtelet acquainted the King that he could not answer for the French Guards. Châtelet, who, from his hot arrogant temper, I should have thought would have been one of the proudest opposers of the people, is suspected to lean to them. In short, Marshal Broglio is appointed commander-in-chief, and is said to have sworn on his sword, that he will not sheathe it till he has plunged it into the heart of 'ce gros banquier Genevois.' I cannot reconcile this with Necker's stay at Versailles. That he is playing a deep game is certain. It is reported that Madame Necker tastes previously everything he swallows. A vast camp is forming round Paris; but the army is mutinous – the tragedy may begin on the other side. They do talk of an engagement at Metz, where the French troops, espousing the popular cause, were attacked by two German regiments, whom the former cut to pieces. The Duke and Duchess of Devonshire, who were at Paris, have thought it prudent to leave it; and my cousin, Mr. Thomas Walpole, who is near it, has just written to his daughters, that he is glad to be out of the town, that he may make his retreat easily.

Thus, you see the crisis is advanced far beyond orations, and wears all the aspect of civil war. For can one imagine that the whole nation is converted at once, and in some measure without provocation from the King, who, far from enforcing the prerogative like Charles the First, cancelled the despotism obtained for his grandfather by the Chancellor Maupeou, has exercised no tyranny, and has shown a disposition to let the constitution be amended. It did want it indeed; but I fear the present want of temper grasps at so much, that they defeat their own purposes; and where loyalty has for ages been the predominant characteristic of a nation, it cannot be eradicated at once. Pity will soften the tone of the moment; and the nobility and clergy have more interest in wearing a royal than a popular yoke; for great lords and high-priests think the rights of mankind a defalcation of their privileges. No man living is more devoted to liberty than I am; yet blood is a terrible price to pay for it!"

Certain letters vividly conjure up contemporary events, epito-mise or mark the end of an era; such letters are these written in 1789. They paint a picture of Paris at the time of the Revolution. Walpole knew the city well and his horror is more poignant because of this; the contrast between Versailles and Richmond or Strawberry Hill is most marked and is heightened by the day to day account of activities going on around him.

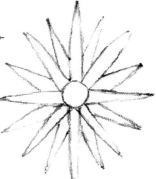

"To Henry Seymour Conway,   Strawberry Hill, Wednesday night
    (The date of this letter is 15 July 1789 although not given by Walpole)
I write a few lines only to confirm the truth of much of what you will read in the papers from Paris. Worse may already be come, or is expected every hour.

    Mr. Mackenzie and Lady Betty called on me before dinner, after the post was gone out; and he showed me a letter from the Duke of Dorset and the Duchess of Devonshire, the latter of whom was leaving Paris directly. Necker had been dismissed, and was thought to be set out for Geneva. Breteuil, who was at his country-house, had been sent for to succeed him. Paris was in an uproar; and, after the couriers had left it, firing of cannon was heard for four hours together. That must have been from the Bastile, as probably the 'Tiers Etat' were not so provided. It is shocking to imagine what may have happened in such a thronged city ! One of the couriers was stopped twice or thrice, as supposed to pass from the King; but redeemed himself by pretending to be despatched by the 'Tiers Etat'. Madame de Calonne told Dutens, that the newly encamped troops desert by hundreds.

    Here seems the egg to be hatched, and imagination runs away with the idea. I may fancy I shall hear of the King and Queen leaving Versailles, like Charles the First, and then skips imagination six-and-forty years lower, and figures their fugitive Majesties taking refuge in this country. I have besides another idea. If the Bastile conquers, still is it impossible, considering the general spirit in the country, and the numerous fortified places in France, but some may be seized by the 'dissidents' and whole provinces be torn from the Crown? On the other hand, if the King prevails, what heavy despotism will the 'Etats', by their want of temper and moderation, have drawn on their country! They might have obtained many capital points, and have removed great oppression. No French monarch will ever summon 'Etats' again, as this moment has been thrown away.

    Though I have stocked myself with such a set of visions for the event either way, I do not pretend to foresee what will happen. Penetration argues from reasonable probabilities; but chance and folly are apt to contradict calculation, and hitherto they seem to have full scope for action. One hears of no genius on either side, nor do symptoms of any appear. There will perhaps: such times and tempests bring forth, at least bring out, great men. I do not take the Duke of Orléans or Mirabeau to be built 'du bois dont on les fait' no, nor Monsieur Necker. He may be a great traitor, if he made the confusion designedly: but it is a woeful evasion, if the promised financier slips into a black politician! I adore liberty, but I would bestow it as honestly as I could; and a civil war, besides being a game of chance, is paying a very dear price for it.

For us, we are in most danger of a deluge; though I wonder we so frequently complain of long rains. The saying about St. Swithin is a proof of how often they recur; for proverbial sentences are the children of experience, not of prophecy. Good night! In a few days I shall send you a beautiful little poem from the Strawberry press."

❖ ❖ ❖

George Nicol visited Strawberry Hill in July of 1790 with John Boydell. Boydell, mainly known today for his collection of paintings, later produced as prints, illustrating Shakespeare's plays, had arranged for the engraving of some of the Houghton paintings of Robert Walpole including a self portrait of Frans Hals, engraved by Michel and published in 1777 embellished by the Orford coat of arms.

"To George Nicol,   Strawberry Hill, 6 July 1790
It gives me great pleasure to hear, Sir, that my house and collection entertained you so well. They have many visitants, for I refuse none, though frequently not very conveniently; yet I never regret that disturbance, when it is not idle curiosity and the fondness for making a party that draws spectators hither – but to persons of taste and knowledge like you and your friends, I am happy to show the collection myself.

You express so much kind satisfaction, Sir, in what you did see, that I will venture to say you saw my assemblage of curious trifles very imperfectly. I am not only afraid of tiring my company, for a virtuoso is apt to set a value on things that appear errant baubles to others, but from my age and lameness it is impossible for me to go through the whole collection even with a small number of persons: but if you will give me another day alone and take a bed here, at your leisure, I flatter myself I could amuse you for good part of the time, and even with what you are a better judge of than I am, a few singular books, which I had not time to produce last week.

This is but a preface, Sir, to the gratitude I owe you for the very obliging offers of service you make me – but as you have so much modesty yourself, I hope you will excuse my saying that you wound mine by the far too civil terms in which you speak of my very shallow literary merit, which has never aimed at more than amusing myself. There was a time when I should have been proud of receiving both assistance and information from you – now, at near seventy-four, I have neither the presumption to look forwards to duration, nor the vanity to imagine that old age, additionally enfeebled by between thirty and forty years of gout, is fit for anything but repose. My best wisdom has consisted in forming a baby-house full of playthings for my second childhood, and I fear they do me more honour, especially as they amused you, than what Pope so well has called

> the rattles of the Man or Boy

I am extremely thankful, Sir, both to you and Mr Lodge for his offer of inspection of the roll exhibiting a portrait of Richard III. I shall be glad to see it, but will certainly not trespass on his too great indulgence – on the contrary, when I come to town, I will wait on him and look at it at the College of Arms. I imagine it is a duplicate of one drawn by Rous of Warwick, which was in the possession of the late Duke of Mancester, and I suppose is still at Kimbolton. The late Duke was so good as to lend it to me, and I had some of the portraits not only copied but engraved for a second edition of my *Historic Doubts*, though I have been too indolent to put my intention in practice. I will show them to you, when I have the pleasure of seeing you here again .....

You say you are not apt to write long letters (the greater obligation to me) I fear I am apt to write long ones; an old man and an old scribbling pen are subject to babble ....."

*I*n 1791, aged seventy four, Walpole succeeded his nephew and became the 4th Earl of Orford, inheriting Houghton Hall in Norfolk, his father's expensively built classical mansion; he preferred his 'gingerbread castle'. He never took his seat in the House of Lords. He found the Earldom brought with it more responsibility than pleasure although he enjoyed the title itself. The last years of his life were not happy ones; so many friends had died, he no longer trusted some of his servants, his body was full of pain and Strawberry Hill, which he visited less often, gave him less pleasure and acquired an air of neglect.

"To the Miss Berrys,   Berkeley Square, 23 August 1791
..... On Monday was the boat-race. I was in the great room at the Castle, with the Duke of Clarence, Lady Di., Lord Robert Spencer, and the House of Bouverie, to see the boats start from the bridge to Thistleworth, and back to a tent erected on Lord Dysart's meadow, just before Lady Di's windows; whither we went to see them arrive, and where we had breakfast. For the second heat, I sat in my coach on the bridge; and did not stay for the third. The day had been coined on purpose, with my favourite south-east wind. The scene, both up the river and down, was what only Richmond upon earth can exhibit. The crowds on these green velvet meadows and on the shores, the yachts, barges, pleasure and small boats, and the windows and gardens lined with spectators, were so delightful, that when I came home from that vivid show, I thought Strawberry looked as dull and solitary as a hermitage. At night there was a ball at the Castle, and illuminations, with the Duke's cypher, etc., in coloured lamps, as were the houses of his Royal Highness's tradesmen. I went again in the evening to the French ladies on the Green, where there was a bonfire; but, you may believe, not to the ball ....."

❖❖❖

Hannah More was a correspondent for whom Walpole had a great respect. She was widely read, known for her wit and compassion, and like Walpole she was an early advocate for the abolition of slavery.

"To Miss Hannah More,   Strawberry Hill, 21 August, 1792
My dear Saint Hannah,
..... this second massacre of Paris has exhibited horrors that even surpass the former. even the Queen's women were butchered in the Tuileries, and the tigers chopped off the heads from the dead bodies, and tossed them into the flames of the palace. The tortures of the poor King and Queen, from the length of their duration, surpass all example; and the brutal insolence with which they were treated on the 10th, all invention. They were dragged

through the Place Vendome to see the statue of Louis the
Fourteenth in fragments, and told it was to be the King's
fate; and he, the most harmless of men, was told he is a
monster; and this after three years of sufferings. King,
and Queen, and children, were shut up in a room,
without nourishment, for twelve hours. One who was a
witness has come over, and says he found the Queen
sitting on the floor, trembling like an aspen in every
limb, and her sweet boy the Dauphin asleep against
her knee! She has not one woman to attend her that
she ever saw, but a companion of her misery, the King's
sister, an heroic virgin saint, who, on the former irruption
into the palace, flew to and clung to her brother, and being
mistaken for the Queen, and the hellish fiends wishing to
murder her, and somebody aiming to undeceive them, she said, 'Ah! ne les
détrompez pas'! was not that sentence the sublime of innocence? But why
do I wound your thrilling nerves with the relation of such horrible scenes?
Your blackmanity must allow some of its tears to these poor victims. For my
part, I have an abhorrence of politics, if one can so term these tragedies,
which make one harbour sentiments one naturally abhors; but can one refrain
without difficulty from exclaiming such wretches should be exterminated?
They have butchered hecatombs of Swiss, even to porters in private houses,
because they often are, and always are called, Le Suisse. Think on fifteen
hundred persons, probably more, butchered on the 10th, in the space of
eight hours. Think on premiums voted for the assassination of several princes,
and do not think that such execrable proceedings have been confined to
Paris; no, Avignon, Marseilles, etc., are still smoking with blood! Scarce the
Alecto of the North, the legislatress and the usurper of Poland, has occasioned
the spilling of larger torrents!

I am almost sorry that your letter arrived at this crisis; I cannot help
venting a little of what haunts me. But it is better to thank providence for
the tranquillity and happiness we enjoy in this country, in spite of the
philosophising serpents we have in our bosom, the Paines, the Tookes, and
the Woolstonecrafts. I am glad you have not read the tract of the last-
mentioned writer. I would not look at it, though assured it contains neither
metaphysics nor politics; but as she entered the lists on the latter, and borrowed
her title from the demon's book, which aimed at spreading the wrongs of
men, she is excommunicated from the pale of my library. We have had
enough of new systems, and the world a great deal too much ....."

✦✦✦

The villa from the following letter is Lacy House, Isleworth.

"To Lady Ossory,   Berkeley Square, 26 December 1793
You are too good, Madam, in giving yourself the trouble of inquiring after my decays. As they are not so rapid as I might reasonably expect, they are not worthy of interesting anybody; and, while seldom attended by pain, I have little cause for complaint.

I am glad Lord and Lady Warwick are pleased with their new villa: it is a great favourite with me. In my brother's time I used to sit with delight in the bow-window in the great room, for besides the lovely scene of Richmond, with the river, park, and barges, there is an incessant ferry for foot passengers between Richmond and Isleworth, just under the Terrace; and on Sundays Lord Shrewsbury pays for all the Catholics that come to his chapel from the former to the latter, and Mrs. Keppel has counted an hundred in one day, at a penny each. I have a passion for seeing passengers, provided they do pass; and though I have the river, the road, and two foot-paths before my Blue Room at Strawberry, I used to think my own house dull whenever I came from my brother's. Such a partiality have I for moving objects, that in advertisements of country-houses I have thought it a recommendation when there was a N.B. of three stage coaches pass by the door every day. On the contrary, I have an aversion to a park, and especially for a walled park, in which the capital event is the coming of cows to water. A park-wall with ivy on it and fern near it, and a back parlour in London in summer, with a dead creeper and a couple of sooty sparrows, are my strongest ideas of melancholy solitude. A pleasing melancholy is a very august personage, but not at all good company. I am still worse, when I have so little to say; but indeed I only meant this as a letter of thanks for your kind inquiries after my lame hand, of which my surgeon has taken leave this morning."

"To Lady Ossory,   Sunday, 15 January, 1797
My dear madam,
You distress me infinitely by showing my idle notes, which I cannot conceive can amuse anybody. My old-fashioned breeding impels me every now and then to reply to the letters you honour me with writing, but in truth very unwillingly, for I seldom can have anything particular to say; I scarce go out of my own house, and then only to two or three very private places, where I see nobody that really knows anything, and what I learn comes from newspapers, that collect intelligence from coffee-houses; consequently what I neither believe nor report. At home I see only a few charitable elders,

except about forescore nephews and nieces of various ages, who are each brought to me about once a year, to stare at me as the Methusalem of the family, and they can only speak of their own contemporaries, which interest me no more than if they talked of their dolls, or bats and balls. Must not the result of all this, Madam, make me a very entertaining correspondent? And can such letters be worth showing? or can I have any spirit when so old and reduced to dictate? Oh, my good Madam, dispense with me from such a task, and think how it must add to it to apprehend such letters being shown. Pray send me no more such laurels, which I desire no more than their leaves when decked with a scrap of tinsel, and stuck on Twelfth-cakes that lie on the shop-boards of pastry-cooks at Christmas: I shall be quite content with a sprig of rosemary thrown after me, when the parson of the parish commits my dust to dust. Till then, pray, Madam, accept the resignation of
    Your ancient servant,"

This last letter was dictated by Walpole six weeks before his death, and transcribed by Kirgate. It is signed 'O'.

❖ ❖ ❖

Throughout his life at Strawberry Hill Horace Walpole kept his friends informed, through his letters, about the way his Castle was progressing. It is clear that he frequently exaggerated how quickly the the work was being completed, or how slowly the workmen moved, depending on his mood. Whenever he thought of a way in which the house might be improved he wrote to his friends, told them his ideas for changing the tiny villa into a Gothic Castle, and then repeated the information in further letters to other friends; he knew the value of publicity. Each time he wrote, the Castle became more firmly established in people's minds, yet in the interior only the public space from the Front Door to the Armoury and Library were truly Gothic; but this was unimportant. His visitors, whether coming by invitation or ticket, arrived believing they would see a Gothic Castle, and went home marvelling; a Gothic Castle was what they had found.

In the letters describing the building of Strawberry Hill Walpole created a picture of a life that was full of fun, busy, gentle, community orientated but surrounded by tiresome local problems and set-backs. These domestic letters are in startling contrast to the great events taking place at home and abroad: the Gordon riots in London, the French Revolution, the American War of Independence.

He knew and entertained at Strawberry Hill those who formed 18th century policy, he listened, recorded the gossip and relayed what he had heard through his letters. They have become not just a chronicle of building or a diary of events but a means by which the 20th century reader can participate in the pleasures and problems of life in the country as though they were part of 18th century Twickenham society. This is the written legacy of the letters describing the building of Strawberry Hill; the visible legacy is the house itself, complete with Gothic towers and battlements, still standing after 300 years.

ACKNOWLEDGEMENTS

✦ ✦ ✦

I wish to express my thanks to: Professor John Wilton-Ely for reading the manuscript, making valuable suggestions, and for his enthusiastic support; Anthony Beckles Willson for his interest and for reading a section of manuscript; John Iddon for introducing me to Strawberry Hill, and for reading the manuscript; Jackie Latham for checking the text; Louise Leates for reading a section of manuscript and for giving advice on porcelain; Iain McKillop for providing an artist's insight into the building plan, for his advice, and for reading the manuscript; Lisa Oestreicher for information from her research on the Hall Staircase; Dr. Michael Peover for use of his research, advice, and information on the glass; Joan Samuel for her invaluable assistance in reading the manuscript and preparing the index; Ian West for information on the shutters.

My thanks also go to: Yale University Press for use of material from the The Yale Edition of Horace Walpole's Correspondence, volumes 1-48, edited by W. S. Lewis, and permission to quote from the Correspondence; Richard Williams of the Lewis Walpole Library, Farmington, Connecticut, for his help and for granting the artist permission to copy the portrait of Horace, painted by Ramsay, which hangs in, and is owned by, the Library; the House Guides of Strawberry Hill, all of whom have contributed through their research to an increased knowledge and awareness of Horace Walpole and Strawberry Hill; Dr. Naylor and the staff of St. Mary's University College for their long suffering support and assistance and for granting permission to the artist to paint and draw within Strawberry Hill.

I should also like to thank the many writers on Walpole and his house, listed and unlisted in the bibliography, whose work I have found invaluable.

Lastly, I wish to thank Sylvia Jones for drawings which encapsulate the enduring quality and charm of Strawberry Hill.

Anna Chalcraft, May 1998

Brief Guide to Correspondents, Friends, Servants and Craftsmen Mentioned in the Letters or Text
listed under their most frequently used titles or names

✦ ✦ ✦

Robert ADAM: (1728-1792), architect, employed to design the Round Drawing Room of Strawberry Hill.

Lady AILESBURY: (1721-1803), Caroline Campbell, m. first, Charles, Earl of Ailesbury, second, Henry Seymour (Seymore) Conway; mother of Anne Seymour Damer.

ASCIOTTI: Commissioned by Walpole to obtain 16th and 17th Century Netherlandish/Flemish glass for Strawberry Hill.

Tom BARNEY: Horace Walpole's old servant who accompanied him on the Grand Tour.

Lady Diana BEAUCLERC: (1734-1808), Diana Spencer, m. first, Viscount Bolingbroke, divorced 1768, second, Topham Beauclerc(k), executed drawings for *The Mysterious Mother* and designs for Josiah Wedgwood.

Richard BENTLEY: (1708-1782), Member of Committee of Taste, draughtsman of early building plan of Strawberry Hill, chimney-piece designer for Strawberry Hill, illustrator of Gray's poems.

BERRY family: Father, Robert (d. 1817); 2 daughters, Mary (1763-1852) and Agnes (1764-1852); all were friends of Walpole and lived at Little Strawberry Hill.

Thomas BROMWICH: (d.1787), Paper stainer, decorator, provided Strawberry Hill wallpapers and papier-mâché for Staircase, Pink Room, Gallery, Green Closet and garrets between c1748-1762. Paid £115.0.0. for Gallery ceiling.

Mrs. CHENEVIX: (d.1755), Elizabeth, toywoman or toy-shop keeper of the Golden Gate, Charing Cross; she rented Chopp'd Straw Hall immediately prior to Walpole.

CLERMONT: (1717-1807), Jean-Francois, French artist employed to paint Library ceiling; paid £73.10.0.

John CHUTE: (1701-1776), member of the Committee of Taste, inherited the Vyne in 1754. Gentleman architect, great friend, designed much of Strawberry Hill including the West Front and the Library.

Rev. William COLE: (1714-1782), Clergyman, antiquarian, friend.

CONWAY: (1719-1795), The Hon. Henry Seymour (Seymore) Conway, cousin, friend; Field Marshal, Secretary of State,

Anne DAMER:	M.P. m. Lady Ailesbury, father of Anne Seymour Damer. (1748-1828), Anne Seymour (Seymore) Conway, daughter of Lady Ailesbury and Henry Seymour Conway, m. Hon. John Damer. Sculptress, friend of Berrys, spent much of her childhood at Strawberry Hill and on Walpole's death inherited £2,000 a year and a life-tenancy of the house.
Mme. du DEFFAND:	(d. 1780), Marie de Vichy Chamrond, Marquise. Blind, much older than Walpole, a great friend visited by him in Paris.
Cornelius DIXON:	Paper stainer from Norwich, worked at Strawberry Hill repainting Hall paper c1791.
James ESSEX:	(1722-1784), architect, builder; designed the Beauclerc Tower, Gothic Gates and New Offices of Strawberry Hill.
FAVRE:	Head man servant at Walpole's house in Arlington Street; also worked at Strawberry Hill.
Thomas GRAY:	(1716-1771), poet, Walpole's companion on the Grand Tour 1739-1741. Author of 'Ode on the Death of a Favourite Cat, Drowned in a Tub of Gold Fishes' written about Selima, Walpole's cat, and of the 'Elegy Written in a Country Churchyard'.
Sir William HAMILTON:	(1730-1803), Statesman, diplomat, antiquary, envoy to Naples 1764-1800; Involved in excavations of Herculaneum and Pompeii, supplied many excavated objects for Strawberry Hill.
HARRY:	Henry Jones, manservant, steward and butler to Walpole between 1752-1762.
Lord HERTFORD:	(1718-1794), Francis Seymour (Seymore) Conway, Earl of Hertford, brother to Henry Seymour Conway, Ambassador to Paris.
Lady HERVEY:	(1700-1768), Mary Lepell, m. John, Baron Hervey of Ickworth.
Henrietta HOWARD:	(1681-1767), Countess of Suffolk, Mistress of George 11, owner of Marble Hill, friend and neighbour of Walpole.
Thomas KIRGATE:	(1734-1810), Printer at Strawberry Hill Press from 1765, became secretary and librarian to Walpole.
W. S. LEWIS:	(1859-1979), Wilmarth Sheldon Lewis, authority on Walpole, founder of the Lewis Walpole Library at Farmington, Connecticut, a research library for English 18th century studies, now owned by Yale University. Collector of Walpoliana, author of many works on Walpole, Editor of the 'Yale Edition of Horace Walpole's Correspondence'.

Sir Horace MANN:	(1706-1786), Horatio, English Resident in Florence, friend and distant cousin to Walpole, supplied many objects for Strawberry Hill. Lifelong correspondent of almost 1800 letters.
MARGARET Young:	Housekeeper at Strawberry Hill; worked there from 1760-1786.
Rev. William MASON:	(1725-1797), Clergyman, friend, biographer of Gray.
George MONTAGU:	(c1713- 1780), M.P., Friend, correspondent of the early years.
MUNTZ:	(1727-1798), Johann Heinrich, topographical artist and designer, worked as artist in residence at Strawberry Hill.
George MURRAY:	(d.1761), Master Carver and Sculptor. Worked on Little Parlour Chimney-piece for which he was paid £8.0.0.
Lady OSSORY:	(c1738-1804), Hon. Anne Liddell, m. first, Duke of Grafton, second, John Fitzpatrick, second Earl of Upper Ossory.
PALMER:	Glazier of St. Martin's Lane, provider of coloured glass mosaic surrounding the roundels at Strawberry Hill.
James PEARSON:	(d.1805), Glass painter of 'The Cobbler whistling to a caged bird' in the Great Parlour.
William PECKITT:	or Pecket, (1731-1795), glass painter and glazier from York. Worked at Strawberry Hill on Round Drawing Room windows, Long Gallery, and Star skylight of golden glass in Tribune, for which he was paid £34.14.0., also armorial glass in the Great North Bedchamber.
Thomas PITT:	(1737-1793), Baron Camelford, M.P. Designed, with Chute, ornament for the Tribune and Long Gallery and the Long Gallery chimney-piece.
William PRICE:	'The Younger'. Glass painter, worked at Strawberry Hill on the Holbein Chamber, Tribune and possibly the Beauclerc Closet.
Alexander POPE:	(1688-1744), poet, satirist, Twickenham resident.
Duchess of QUEENSBURY:	(1701-1777), Catherine Hyde, Neighbour of Walpole.
William ROBINSON:	(c1720-1777), architect, Secretary to the Board of Works, Clerk of Works to the Committee of Taste, designed the Blue Breakfast Room chimney-piece.
George SELWYN:	(1717-1791), friend, wit, joker. Gave Walpole armorial glass for the Little Parlour of Strawberry Hill.
Lord STRAFFORD:	(1722 1791), William Wentworth, 2nd Earl Strafford, friend.
TUDOR:	Paper stainer employed to paint Hall of Strawberry Hill after Bentley fled to Jersey.

C. H. WILLIAMS: (1708-1759), Sir Charles Hanbury, friend, wit.

James WYATT: (1746-1813), architect, builder of the New Offices at Strawberry Hill.

A Select Bibliography
***

Alexander, D.,   Affecting Moments, Prints of English Literature made in the
                          Age of Romantic Sensibility, 1775-1800, (York, 1993).

Anon.   A Catalogue of the Contents of Strawberry Hill, for George
                          Robins, auctioneer, (London, 1842).

Anon.   Aedes Strawberrianae, Names of Purchasers and the Prices
                          to the Sale Catalogue of the Collections of Art and Vertu, at
                          Strawberry Hill, (London, 1842).

Anon.   Ambulator: or A Pocket Companion in a Tour Round
                          London, (London, 1800).

Batey, M.,   Horace Walpole as Modern Garden Historian, (Garden
                          History: The Journal of the Garden History Society, Spring
                          1991).

Beckles Willson, A.,   Strawberry Hill: A History of the Neighbourhood,
                          (Twickenham, 1991).

Brewer, J.,   The Pleasures of the Imagination, (Harper Collins, London,
                          1997).

Calloway, S., Snodin, M., Wainwright, C.,
                          Horace Walpole and Strawberry Hill, (Exhibition Catalogue,
                          Orleans House Gallery, Richmond Upon Thames, 1980).

Cauwelaert, M. van,   Vitraux, (Musees Royaux d'Art et d'Histoire, Brussels, 1990).

Clarke, K.,   The Gothic Revival, (London, 1928).

Cocke, T.H.,   The Ingenious Mr. Essex, Architect, (Fitzwilliam Museum,
                          Cambridge, 1984).

Crook, J.M.,   Strawberry Hill Revisited, (Country Life, June 7, 14, 21 1973).

Doyle, Rev. J.,   Strawberry Hill, (St. Mary's College, Twickenham, 1972).

Eavis, A., & Peover, M., Horace Walpole's Painted Glass at Strawberry Hill, (The
                          Journal of Stained Glass, Vol. XIX No.3 1994-5).

Fleming, J.,   Adam Gothic, (The Connisseur, October, 1958).

Fothergill, B.,   The Strawberry Hill Set: Horace Walpole and His Circle,
                          (Faber & Faber, London, 1983).

Greenwood, A.,   Horace Walpole's World, (Bell & Sons, London, 1913).

Guillery, P.,   Strawberry Hill: Building and Site: Part One: The Building,
                          (Architectural History, Vol.38, Leeds, 1995).

Gwynn, S.,   The Life of Horace Walpole, (Butterworth, London, 1932).

Halfpenny, W.,   (and others), The Modern Builder's Assistant, (London, 1742).

Halsband, R.,   The Rococco in England: Book Illustrators, mainly Gravelot
                          and Bentley, (Burlington Magazine, 1985).

Hawkins, L.M.,	Anecdotes, Biographical Sketches and Memoirs, (1822).
Hazen, A.T.,	A Bibliography of Horace Walpole, (Yale, New Haven & London, 1948).
Honour, H.,	Horace Walpole, (The British Council through Longmans, London,1957).
Hoskins, L	(ed.), The Papered Wall, (Abrams & Thames & Hudson, London, 1994).
Iddon, J.,	Horace Walpole's Strawberry Hill, (St. Mary's University College, Twickenham, 1996).
Johnstone, Chevalier de,	A Memoir of the 'Forty-Five, (Folio Society, London, 1958).
Judd, G.P.,	Horace Walpole's Memoirs, (Vision, U.S.A., 1960).
Ketton-Cremer, R.,	Horace Walpole, (Longman, London, 1940).
Langley, B.,	Ancient Architecture Restored and Improved,(London, 1742).
Lewis, W.S.,	The Genesis of Strawberry Hill, (Metropolitan Museum Studies, Vol. 5 No. I, 1934-1936).
	Horace Walpole, (New York, 1961).
	ed. The Yale Edition of Horace Walpole's Correspondence, vols. 1-48, (published between 1937 and 1983).
Mayor, A.H.,	A Note on the Prints at Strawberry Hill, Paper, from Horace Walpole Writer, Politician, Connoisseur, (Yale, New Haven & London, 1967).
McKillop, I.M.,	A Chronology of Horace Walpole, (unpublished).
McLeod, B.,	Horace Walpole and Sèvres porcelain: The Collection at Strawberry Hill, (Apollo, January, 1998).
Murray Kendall, P.,	Richard the Third, (Allen & Unwin, London, 1955).
McCarthy, M.,	The Origins of the Gothic Revival, (Yale, New Haven and London, 1987).
Pevsner, N.,	Rococco Gothic: Walpole, Bentley and Strawberry Hill, (Architectural Review, Vol. XCVIII, December 1945).
Peover, M.,	Horace Walpole's Stained Glass, (Country Life, October 26, 1995).
Rosoman, T.,	London Wallpapers, Their Manufacture and Use, (English Heritage, 1992).
Snodin, M.,	Strawberry Hill: Building and Site: Part Two: The Site, (Architectural History, Vol. 38, Leeds, 1995).
Summerson, J.,	Georgian London, (London, 1948).
Toynbee, P.,	Journal of the Printing Office at Strawberry Hill, (Chiswick, London, 1923).
	The Strawberry Hill Accounts, (Oxford, 1927).
Wainwright, C.,	The Romantic Interior, (Yale, New Haven & London, 1989).
Walpole, H.,	The Works of Horatio Walpole, Earl of Orford, (London, 1798).

Watson, F.J.B.,   Walpole and the Taste for French Porcelain in Eighteenth
                      Century England, paper, from Horace Walpole, Writer,
                      Politician and Connoisseur, (Yale, New Haven & London,
                      1967).
Wilton-Ely, J.,   Horace Walpole and the Grand Tour, paper, from Bicentenary
                      Conference, Horace Walpole, Art and Politics, (1997).

GROUND FLOOR

1 Eating room/Great Parlour/
   Refectory
2 Waiting Room/Cool Little
   Hall
3 China Closet
4 Little Parlour
5 Yellow Bedchamber/
   Beauty Room
6 Hall & Staircase
7 Great Cloister
8 Kitchen
9 Servant's Hall (adjacent
   rooms held stores)
10 Oratory
11 Little Cloister
12 Prior's Garden
13 Entrance
14 Front Door

   Rooms 2-6 covered the area
   of Chopp'd Straw Hall

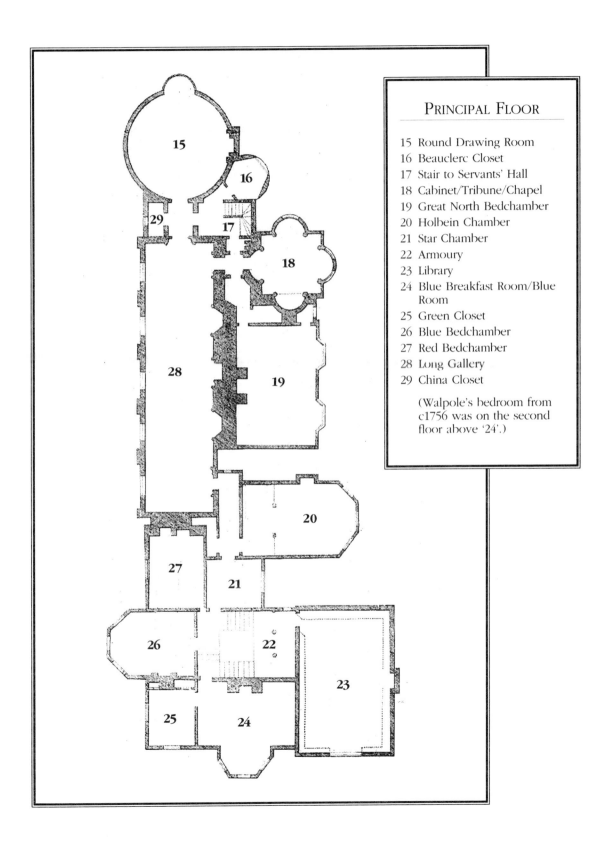

PRINCIPAL FLOOR

15 Round Drawing Room
16 Beauclerc Closet
17 Stair to Servants' Hall
18 Cabinet/Tribune/Chapel
19 Great North Bedchamber
20 Holbein Chamber
21 Star Chamber
22 Armoury
23 Library
24 Blue Breakfast Room/Blue Room
25 Green Closet
26 Blue Bedchamber
27 Red Bedchamber
28 Long Gallery
29 China Closet

(Walpole's bedroom from c1756 was on the second floor above '24'.)

INDEX

❖ ❖ ❖

Accounts, 7
Adam, Robert, 49,70,71,73,91,133
Africa, 18,19
Ailesbury, Lady, 39,48,109,117,133
Ambulator, 8,116,117
Amelia, Princess, 114,115
America, 19,39,40,92,94,113,127
Ancestors, 14,15,23,28,36
Anecdotes of Painting, 50,51,66,74,75,84,106
Antelopes, 29
Antique/Antiquities, 21,30,84,91,95
Archbishop Wareham's tomb – see Canterbury
Ark, 10,42
Arlington Street, 8,16,19,21,22,23,31,37,38,39,
    41,50,53,55,58,70,74,75,76,77,90,95,99
Arthur, tomb of Prince – see Worcester
    Cathedral,
Armoury, 28,34,38,60,61,71,83,120,127
Asciotti, 22,34,133
Asymmetry, 13,25
Auction, 8,68,77

Balloons, 112,113
Balls/Dancing, 41,42,59,68,69124
Balustrade, 29,78
Barney, Tom, 34,133
Bateman, Richard, 22,57
Batoni, 21
Battlements, 14,15,22,27,28,64,128
Beauclerc, Lady Diana, 79,80,89,90,118,124,133
Beauclerc Tower/Closet, 28,86,89,90,91,92
Beauty Room – see Yellow Bedchamber,
Bedford, Grosvenor, 62
Bedchamber/Walpole's from c1756, 77,82,
    109,119
Bentley, Richard, 7,12,13,26,28,29,31,36,37,38,
    39,40,41,42,44,48,50,80,91,133
Bentley, Richard, (Senior), 12,13
Berkeley Square, 99,100,103,106,109,113,119,
    124,126
Berry Family, 117,118,119,124,133
Blue Bedchamber/Walpole's first bedchamber,
    30,38,39,42,76
Blue Breakfast Room/Blue Room, 10,28,30,44,
    71,82,85,91,108,126
Book Presses/cases, 30,36,37
Boydell, John, 122
Bradford, Earl of, 8
British Museum, 23
Bromwich, 38,39,40,41,133

Cabinet – see Tribune,
Caligula, 21,62
Cambridge, 8,12,66,73,89,91,94,95
Canterbury Cathedral, Archbishop Bourchier's
    tomb, 59

Canterbury Cathedral, Archbishop Wareham's
    tomb, 47
Carpenters, 25,63
Carter, John, 62,81
Castle, 7,14,16,22,25,27,28,29,30,31,50,51,54,
    55,61,64,65,67,70,77,83,84,99,110,112,127
Castle of Otranto, The, 7,51,66,72,74,106
Catalogue of Engravers, 51
Catherine, 42
Catherine the Great, 79,112
Catherine wheels & cross-crosslets, 36,47
Ceilings ,17,36,38,42,54,55,59,61,70,78,91,99
Cellini, Benvenuto, 62,83,86
Chambers, 91
Chantilly, 59,69
Chapel – see Tribune,
Chapel in the Wood, 83,84,119
Charing Cross, 9,104
Charles 1, 21,32,46,61,94,120
Charlotte, Queen, 58,65,94
Chatterton, 66,74,96,97,98
Cheesecake House, 19
Chelsea China, 80
Chenevix, Mrs., 9,10,133
Chimney Piece(s), 10,13,25,36,37,38,41,47,50,
    59,60,70,71,73,74,77,78,82,91,106,108,116
China/ceramics, 44,46,68,69,76,78,79,80,81,85,
    89,113,115
China Closet, 34,44,55,81,85,113
Chivalry, 13,28,66,71
Chopp'd Straw Hall, 8,9,10,18,21,24,47,55,71, 97
Christmas, 11,12,127
Chute, John, 7,12,13,15,18,30,36,37,38,53,57,
    59,84,86,88,89,91,133
Chute, John, Bedchamber of – see Red
    Bedchamber,
Classical Style of Architecture, 16,17,19,38
Classicism, 21
Clay, Henry, 116
Clermont, 36,38,39,133
Clive, Kitty, 99,117
Cloisters, 7,22,27,33,47,57,59
Coats of Arms, 16,22,23,28,34,94,100,122
Cole, William, 66,68,71,72,83,89,92,95,96,99,
    106,133
Collection(s), 21,28,47,50,59,61,62,63,78,79,81,
    83,84,86,114,117,122
Committee on/of Taste, 13,24,80
Conway, Henry Seymour, 9,10,15,39,48,56,
    58,64,73,84,90,103,104,107,110,112,114,117,
    121,133
Cool Little Hall – see Waiting Room
Craftsmen, 7,25,26,28,38,44,47,48,63,64,73,
Crusades, 22,36
Cumberland, Duke of, 54,86

Damer, Anne Seymour, 7,8,110,117,119,134
Dancing – see Balls,
Dart, 24,70
Deffand, Madame du, 83,105,106,134
Description of the Villa of Mr. Horace Walpole at Strawberry Hill, near Twickenham/ Catalogue, 7,26,62,78,79,106,116,117
Dixon, Cornelius, 26,134
Dodsley, 50,72
Dogs, 42,61,76,77,105,107,117,119
Drawings, 7,47,90
Dugdale, 70
Duvivier, 80

Earthquakes, 18,19,20,65,85
Eating Room – see Great Parlour
Eccardt, 38
Edward 1V, King, 21,62,71
Edward the Confessor's Tomb – see Westminster Abbey.
English heads, 21,77,78
Engravings – see Prints.
Entertaining, 11,39,75,99,109,110,111,114
Entrance – see Front Door.
Esher Place, 17
Essex, 89,90,91,92,134
Eton, 8,73

Fabrics, 30,50,55,60,71,89
Fan Vault, 17,94
Farm, 10,42,91,114
Favre, 65,70,134
Flemish glass/Netherlandish glass, 22,34
Floods, 10,42,109
Florence, 8,12,29,49,55,56,62,92,113
Food, 9,11,12,43,75,80,82,111,127
France/French, 8,40,56,58,68,69,75,76,79,85, 92,94,105,109,110,114,118,120,121,122, 124,125,127
Francis 1, King, 62,83,84
Front Door & Entrance, 27,46,84,106,127
Furniture, 7,8,21,30,39,46,47,48,50,55,57,60,61, 62,64,70,71,82,86,115,116

Galfridus, 23
Garden, 11,12,15,19,25,29,30,39,42,44,46,48, 56,65,67,68,76,83,84,87,97,117,126
Genealogy, 13,14,15,22,23,78
Genoa, 27,49,82
George I, King, 22,109,113
George II, King, 23,38,50,53,54,56
George III, King, 50,52, (as Prince of Wales), 53,58,59,65,86,94,100,101
George IV, King (as Prince of Wales), 12, 113,114
Gibbons, Grinling, 21,39,62,75
Gingerbread Castle, 88,124
Glass, 22,24,25,30,34,57,59,60,76,83,85
Glaziers, 25,34
Gloomth, 24,25,60,109
Gloucester, Duchess of – see Maria,
Gloucester, Duke of, 86,87,109

Glo(u)cester Cathedral, 32,33,34,44
Gloves of James I, 75
Goldfish, 37,42,46,110
Goldfish tub/Lofty vase, 46,115
Gordon, Lord George, 100,101,102,103,104, 113,127
Gothic Architecture 11,16,17,18,19,22,24,25, 30,31,33,38,78,83,88,92,94,96,99,100,127
Gothic/Gothicism, 13,16,17,25,26,38,61,66,67, 70,83,88,116
Gothic(k), 16,18,22,24,25,26,27,28,31,34,37, 66,67,78,88,91,94,99,117,127
Gothic lanthorn, 28
Gothic Novel/story, 66,67,72
Gothic style/design, 13,16,17,22,24,25,26,27, 34,37,38,39,40,41,47,55,70,78,88,91,94,99, 117,127
Gothic tombs, 7,15,24,26,31,32,33,46,71,73,78, 83,91,99,100
Gout, 53,69,82,103,110
Grand Tour, 8,12,13,21,27,68,76
Gray, Christopher, 45
Gray, Thomas, 8,13,15,21,37,38,39,41,46,50, 60,74,106,134
Great Cloister, 47,49,57,59
Great North Bedchamber, 25,28,79,81,82,83, 85,86,116
Great Parlour/Refectory/Eating Room, 24,27, 28,30,37,38,39,60, 65,71,75,76,85
Green Closet, 13,30,85,109
Grisaille Glass, 22,30
Gunpowder,84,85

Hall, 7,24,25,26,27,29,34,38,40,60,61,82
Ham, 10
Hamilton, Sir William, 73,84,134
Hanoverians, 17
Harcourt, Earl of, 97
Harry, 42,51,64,134
Hawkins, Laetitia Matilda, 56
Henry VIII, King, 39,46,51,93,94,96
Heraldic Glass, 16,60
Heraldry, 13,14,15,16,22,25,30,36,66,88,123
Herculaneum, 21,62,96
Hertford, Lord & Lady, 48,52,65,69,73,104,134
Hervey, Lady, 68,69,134
Hervey, Lord, 23,107
Highwaymen, 37,108,110
Historic Doubts on the Life and Reign of Richard III, 46,71,123
Holbein, 17,47
Holbein Chamber, 46,47,79,85,106,116
Hollar, Wenceslaus, 70
Hotham, Henrietta, 56,65
Houghton Hall, 17,51,122,124
Howard, Henrietta, Countess of Suffolk, 52, 56,57,65,134

Italy, 8,16,21,25,69

Jackson's Venetian Prints, 29

Jacobites, 17,49
Japanning, 47,116
Johnson, Dr, 106,107

Kent, William, 17,33
King's College, Cambridge, 8,94,95
Kingston, 12,29,111
Kirgate, 36,50,103,104,127,134
Kitchen, 10,44,64

Langley, Batty, 18
Lewis, W.S., 23,112,134
Lewis Walpole Library, 4,112
Library, 9,10,14,24,30,36,37,38,39,51,71,72,76,
    85,88, 106,117,125,127
Library Catalogue, 36
Lime Trees, 11,30
Little Cloister, 27,46,47
Little Cottage, 36,106
Little Parlour, 29,38,40,42,76,108,117
Little Strawberry Hill, 99,117,119
London, 10,14,18,20,28,34,50,58,82,85,91,92,
    96,100,102,103,104,105,116,127
Long Gallery, 17,47,49,50,59,60,61,63,64,66,
    70,73,75,81,82,85,94,99,110
Louis, 52,65
Louis XV1 & family, King, 120,121,124,125

Macaulay, 119
Magna Charta, 21,46
Magpie and her Brood,The 56
Main Entrance and Gate, 27,46,51,65,75
Major Charta, 46
Mann, Horace, 8,11,12,13,14,16,18,19,22,23,
    25,29,34,39,47,49,50,55,62,63,76,77,83,84,86,
    88,92,101,105,109,113,135
Marble Hill, 56
Margaret, 64,85,107,109,111,120,135
Maria/Lady Waldegrave/Duchess of
    Gloucester, 56,65,86,87,103,109
Mason, William, 85,99,103,107,135
Meissen, 80
Miller, Sanderson, 30,31
Money,
    7,8,9,22,28,34,35,38,45,47,50,53,57,63,64,69,
    73,77,78,97,108,111,112,118,119,126
Montagu, George, 11,14,28,42,44,46,48,51,53,
    57,64,67,69,70,75,76,77,82,135
More, Hannah, 124
Muntz, 47,48,135
Murray, 38,135
Music, 75,98
Mysterious Mother, The, 89

Neptune, 10
Netherlandish glass – see Flemish glass,
Newcastle, Duke of, 52,54,85
New Offices, 86,89
Newton, Isaac, 10,18
Nicol, George, 122
Noah, 10,42

Old St. Paul's Cathedral, 27,70,91
Oliver, Isaac, 17
Ossory, Lady, 87,88,90,92,96,97,100,107,108,
    109,111,112,115,116,117,119,126,135

Painted Glass, 8,10,15,16,22,24,25,28,29,30,31,
    32,33,34,57,60,61,73,76,84,110
Paintings,
    12,14,21,31,35,37,38,39,44,46,48,51,60,61,62,
    71,74,75,77,89,90,91,108,112,122,123
Palladian, 17,56
Palmer, 34,135
Paper, 7,54,55,57,99,116
Paper stainers/Papermen, 25,26,28,38
Papier-mâché, 7,17,54,55,59,94
Paraclete, 25
Parliament, 17,18,39,41,42,49,85,101,102,104,
    113,124
Paris, 68,69,70,76,83,92,105,112,113,120,121,
    124,125
Patapan, 76
Pearson, 135
Peckitt, William, 73,135
Philip, 111
Pinnacles, 64,116
Pitt, Thomas, 59,80,81,135
Planting, 12,15,42,44,46
Plasterers, 25,38
Pope, Alexander, 9,10,36,56,75,99,106,107,
    123,135
Pope's Grotto, 75,107
Powder-mills, 20,84,85
Po-Yang, 11,37
Pretender, 17,49,51
Price, 30,33,61,135
Prince Arthur's Tomb – see Worcester
    Cathedral,
Printing Press/House, 7,48,50,75
Print Room – see Yellow Bedchamber,
Prints/Engravings, 7,8,13,18,21,24,26,50,51,70,
    73,77,78,106,112,116,122
Prior's screen/ garden, 27,106

Queensbury, Duchess of, 10,135

Radnor, Lord, 17
Raphael, 62,83,86
Red Bedchamber/John Chute's Bedchamber, 30
Refectory – see Great Parlour,
Reynolds, Joshua, 61,107
Richard II, King, 14
Richard III, King, 71,72,73,123
Richmond, 10,12,14,29,65,111,112,116,121,
    124,126
Richmond, Duke & Duchess of, 48,68,101
Ridotto, 20
River Thames, 9,10,11,12,18,29,56,65,76,
    124,126
Robinson, William, 10,13,91,135
Robsart, Ludovic, 36
Robsart, Sir Terry, 29
Rococco, 13,41,48,89

Rome, 17,21,25,49,84,92
Rosette, 76,77,87,119
Rouen, 27,47
Roundels, 22,24,25
Round/Great Tower, 36,39,44,47,49,50,55,70,
71,83,92
Round Room/Bedchamber & Drawing Room,
49,50,71,73,77,81,85,91,115,116
Royal and Noble Authors, 56

St Martin's Lane, 34,80,104
Sale catalogue, 8
Sandford, 24,100
Saracen/Saracen's Head, 10,22,36,47
Scagliola, 73
Seaport in miniature, 29
Selima, 46,115
Selwyn, George, 32,135
Serendipity, 109
Serpentine Wood, 29,
Servants,
18,19,20,27,34,42,52,64,65,70,82,85,88,89,97,
103,104,107,110,111,120,124
Servant's Hall, 64,71
Sèvres,68,79,80
Shakespeare, 17,36,46,71,72,122
Sharawaggi, 19
Shell Bench, 48
Shells, 21,23
Shorter, Catherine, 8,23,39,109
Short Notes, 8
Shutters, 71
Skerrett, Maria, 23
Slavery, 18,124
Sloane, Sir Hans, 23,
Stained glass, 24,34
Star Chamber, 60,110
Staircase, 24,26,27,28,29,38,67
Strafford, Lord, 64,135
Strawberry Hill, (area), 9,11,16,121
Strawberry Hill, (House), 7,8,10,11,12,13,15,
16,17,20,22,24,26,28,29,34,36,37,38,39,40,41,
42,43,44,46,48,50,54,55,56,58,59,66,68,69,70,
71,75,76,77,81,82,83,85,86,88,91,94,99,103,
105,109,110,111,116,119,122,124,126,127,128
Strawberry Hill, (letters from),
10,11,12,14,18,25,28,29,34,42,44,46,47,48,49,
51,56,57,63,64,65,66,67,68,69,72,73,76,77,82,
83,84,86,87,88,89,90,92,96,97,99,101,103,
105,107,108,110,111,112,114,115,116,117,
119,121,122,124
Strawberry Hill Gothic(k), 16,
Strawberry Hill Press also see Printing Press/
House, 7,36,50,56,89,103,111,114,122
Strike, 63,64
Stuart, Lady Louisa, 23

Terrace, 12,29
Terreno, 20
Theatrical effect, 13,22,26,27,51,54,55,61,114
Thieves, 11,37,64,105,108,110
Tickets, 7,111,127

Tombs, 15,24,25,26,27,31,33,54,61,73,78,83,84,
91,99,100
Tonton, 105,107,113,119
Tory,76
Toys, 9,123,127
Tribune/Cabinet/Chapel, 30,47,49,57,59,61,63,
76,85,110
Trinity College, Cambridge, 12,66
Trompe l'oeil, 27,29,46,61,82
Tudor, 26,40,135
Tudors, the, 17,46
Turkey, 11,12,112
Twickenham, 7,8,9,10,13,18,29,36,51,58,64,85,
87,98,128

Vandyck, 33,38
Vertue, 45,47,50,51
Vestibule, 29,34
Victoria and Albert Museum, 62
Visitors, 27,85,109,110,111,114,115,117,122,127

Waiting Room/Cool Little Hall, 27,30
Waldegrave, 2nd Earl, 86
Waldegrave, 7th Earl, 8
Waldegrave, Countess – see Maria,
Wallpaper, 24,26,27,28,29,30,40,41,47,55,60,
61,89
Walpole, George, 3rd Earl of Orford, 112
Walpole, Robert, 8,17,22,23,39,52,92,112,113,
122,124
Walpole, Thomas, 102,120
Washington, George, 39,40
Watercolours, 8,30,44,47,81
Weather, 10,12,13,14,18,19,25,42,64,65,68,85,
87,91,109,110,114,116,122,124
Wedgwood, Josiah, 18,79,80,81,89
West, Benjamin, 77
West Front, 47,49,88
Westminster Abbey/Edward the Confessor's
Tomb, 71,73,84,91,99,100,
Westminster Abbey, King Henry VII Chapel,
54,59,94
White's club, 14,20
Williams,Sir Charles, 10,38,39,136
Windows, 25,29,30,33,34,42,46,57,60,61,65,70,
71,73,78,82,84,85,91
Windsor, 10,22,114
Worcester Cathedral, Prince Arthur's tomb,
26,31,32,40
Workmen, 7,25,28,38,44,47,48,63,64,73,74,127
World,The, 80
Wren, Sir Christopher, 33
Wyatt, 91,136

Yellow Bedchamber/Beauty Room/Print
Room, 30,90,91,107,108
York, Duke of, 51,52,58